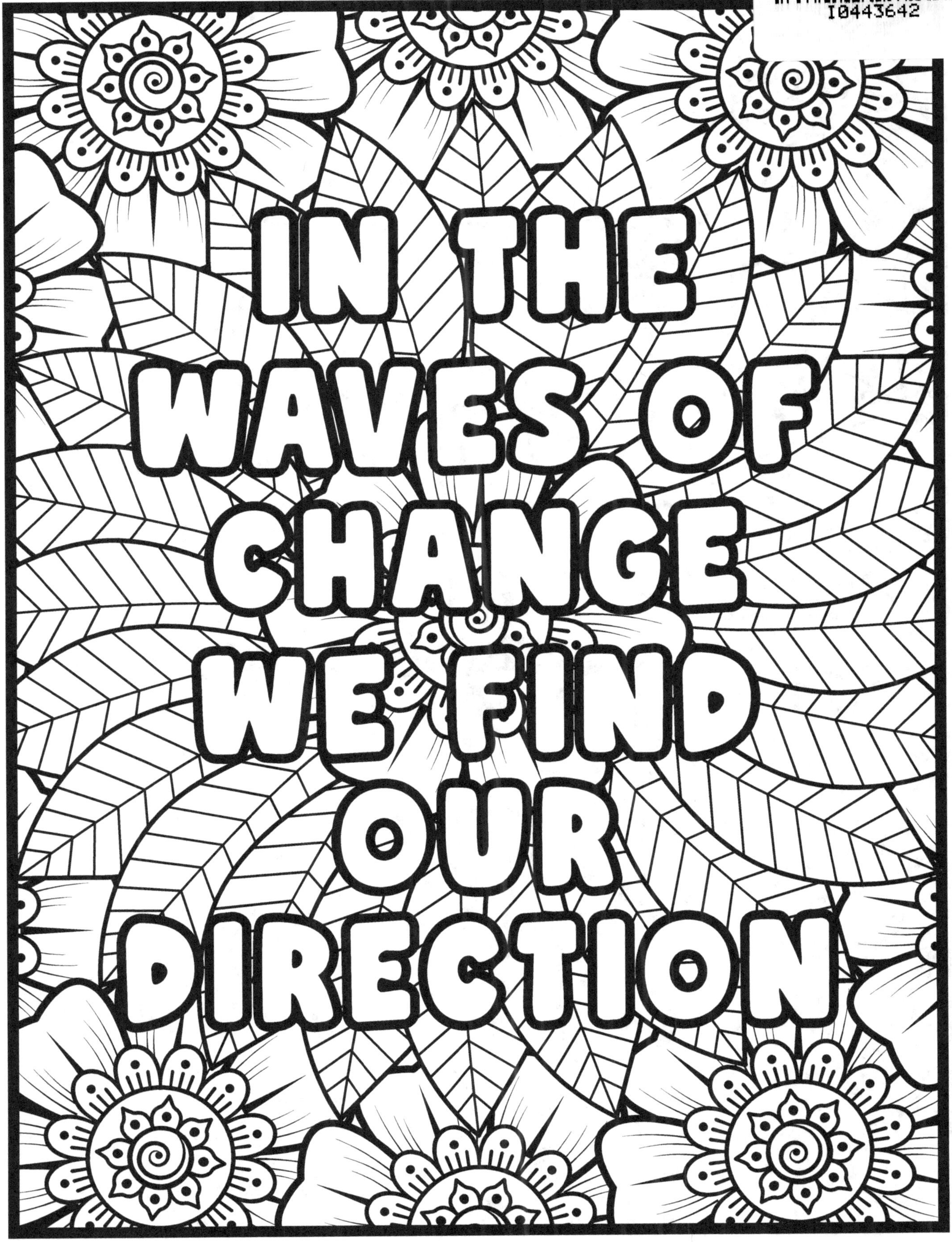
IN THE
WAVES OF
CHANGE
WE FIND
OUR
DIRECTION

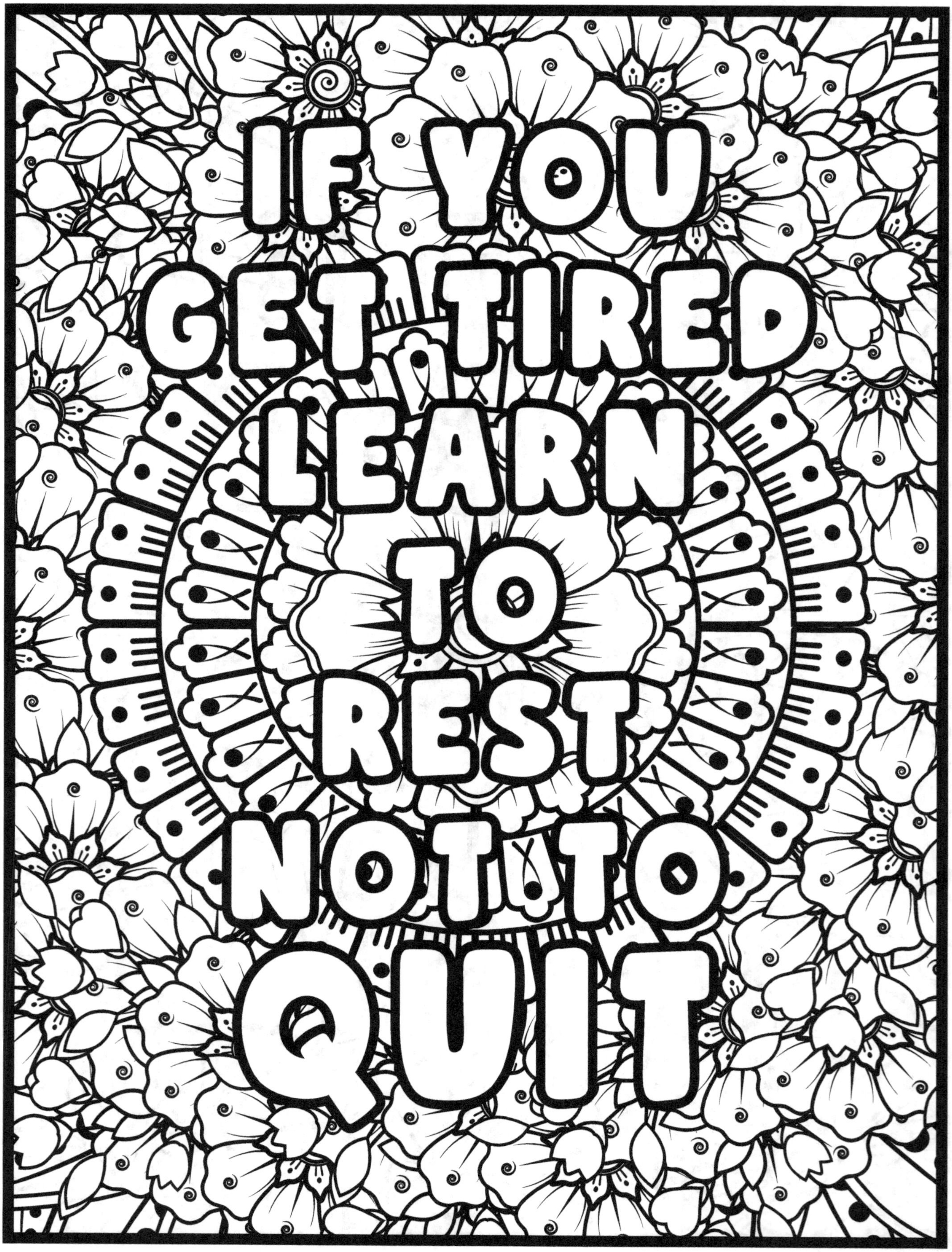
IF YOU
GET TIRED
LEARN
TO
REST
NOT TO
QUIT

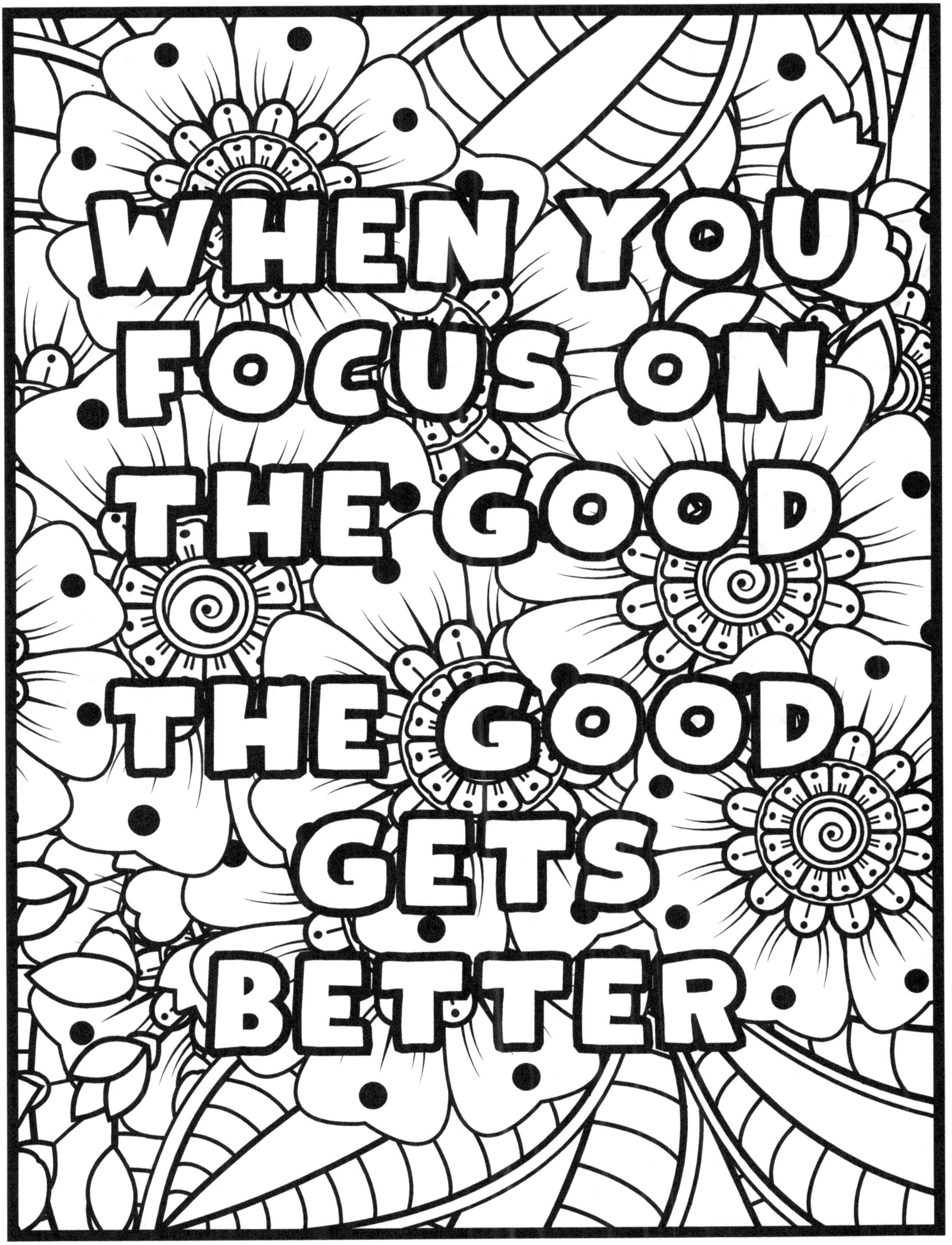
WHEN YOU
FOCUS ON
THE GOOD
THE GOOD
GETS
BETTER

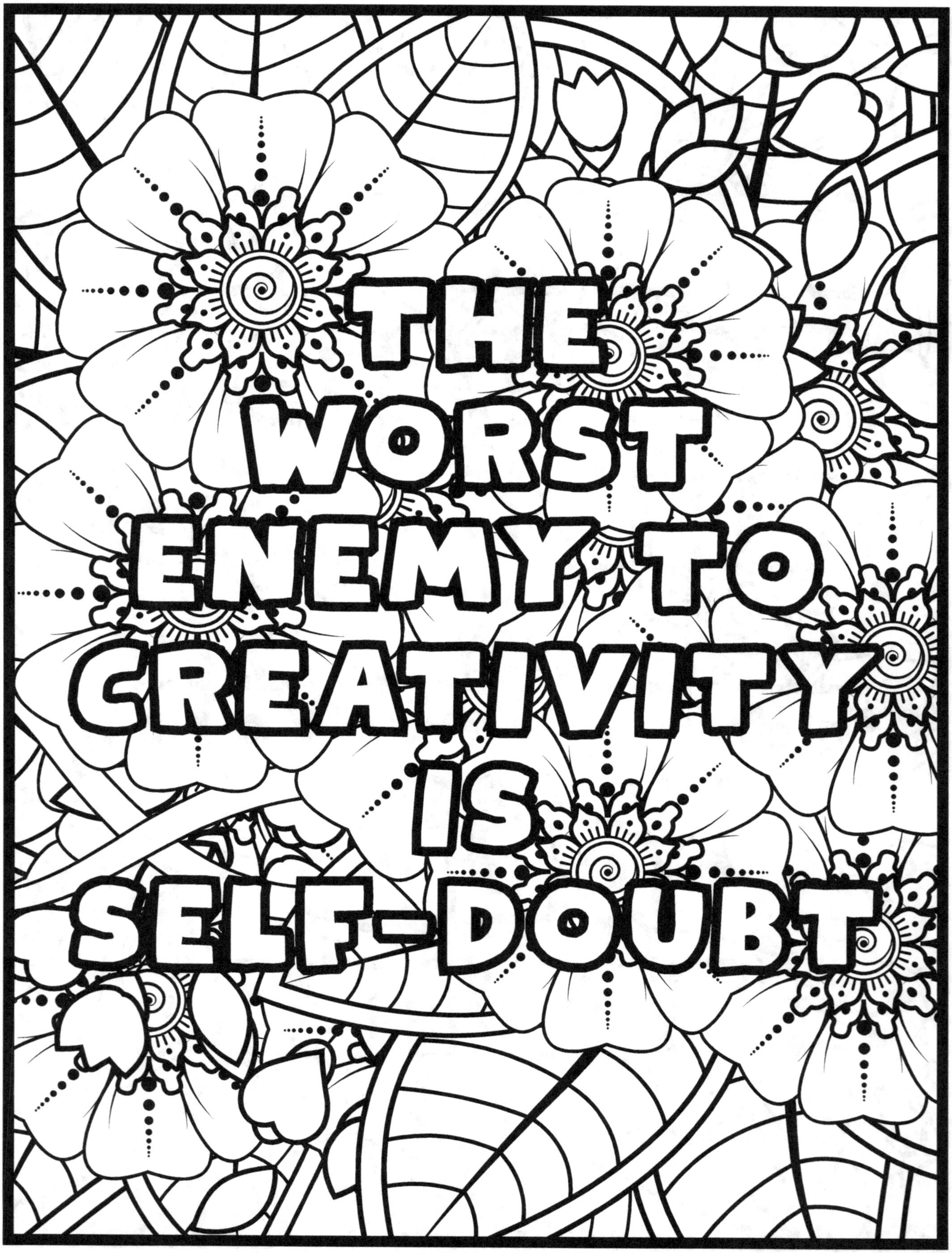
THE
WORST
ENEMY TO
CREATIVITY
IS
SELF-DOUBT

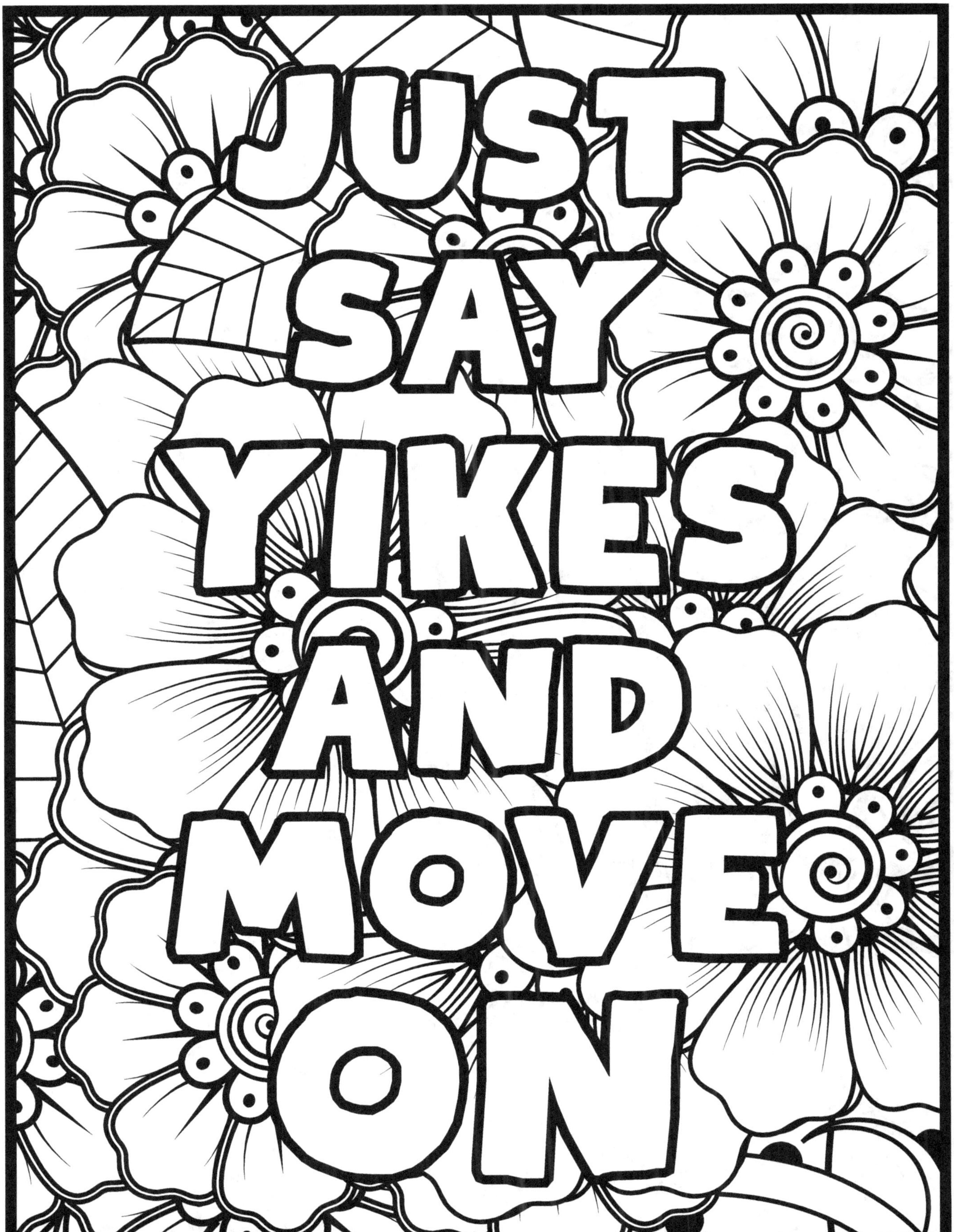
JUST
SAY
YIKES
AND
MOVE
ON

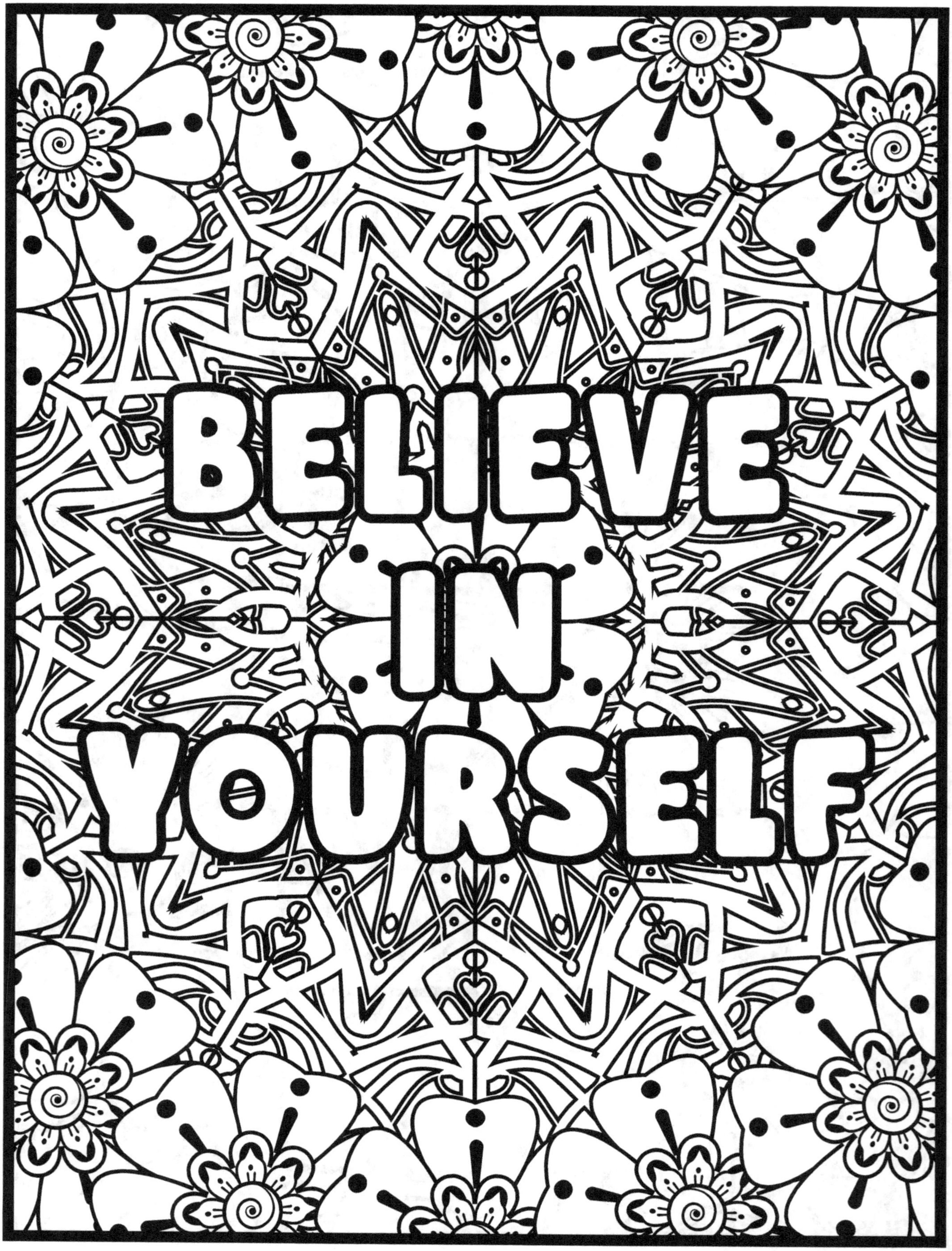
BELIEVE
IN
YOURSELF

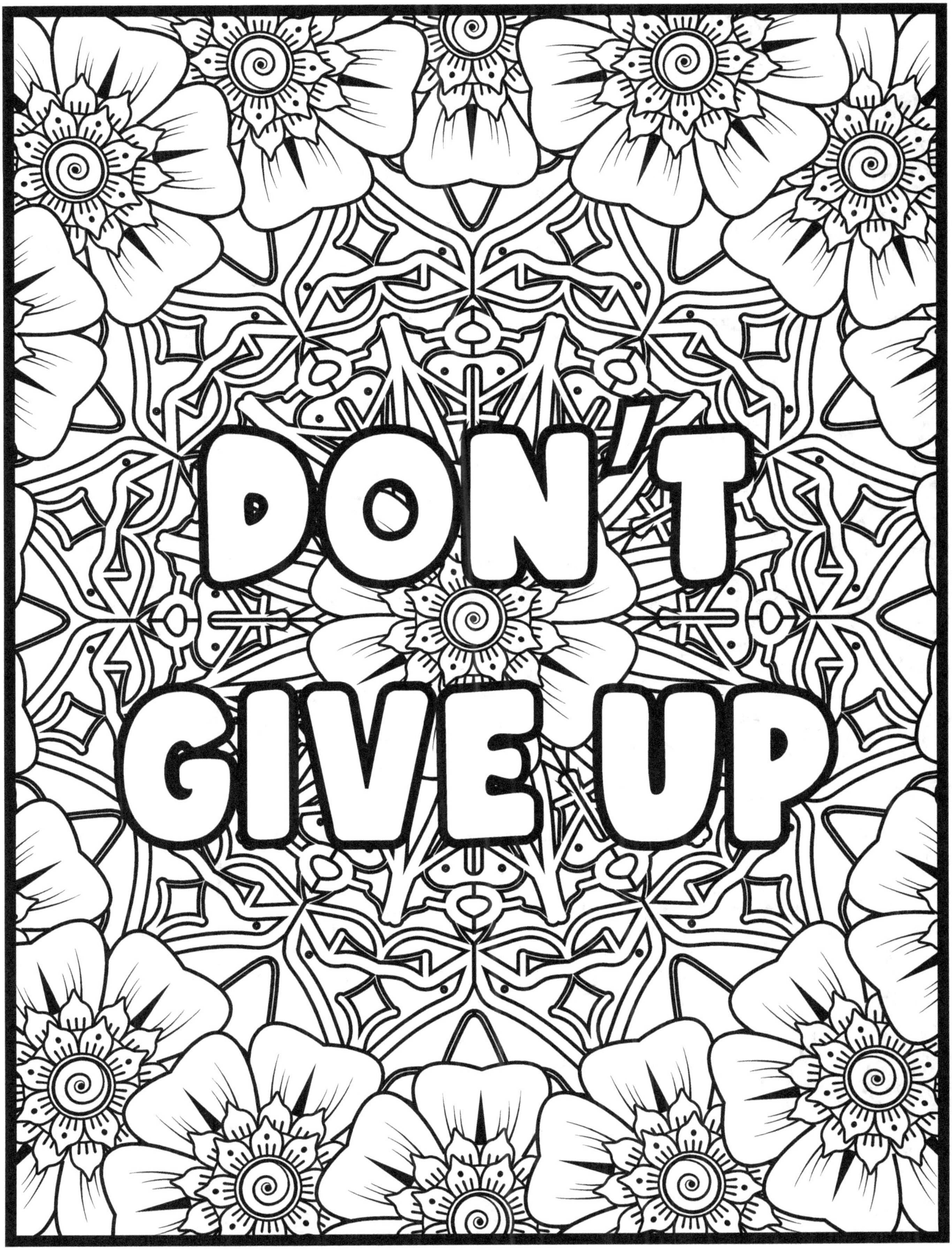
DON'T
GIVE UP

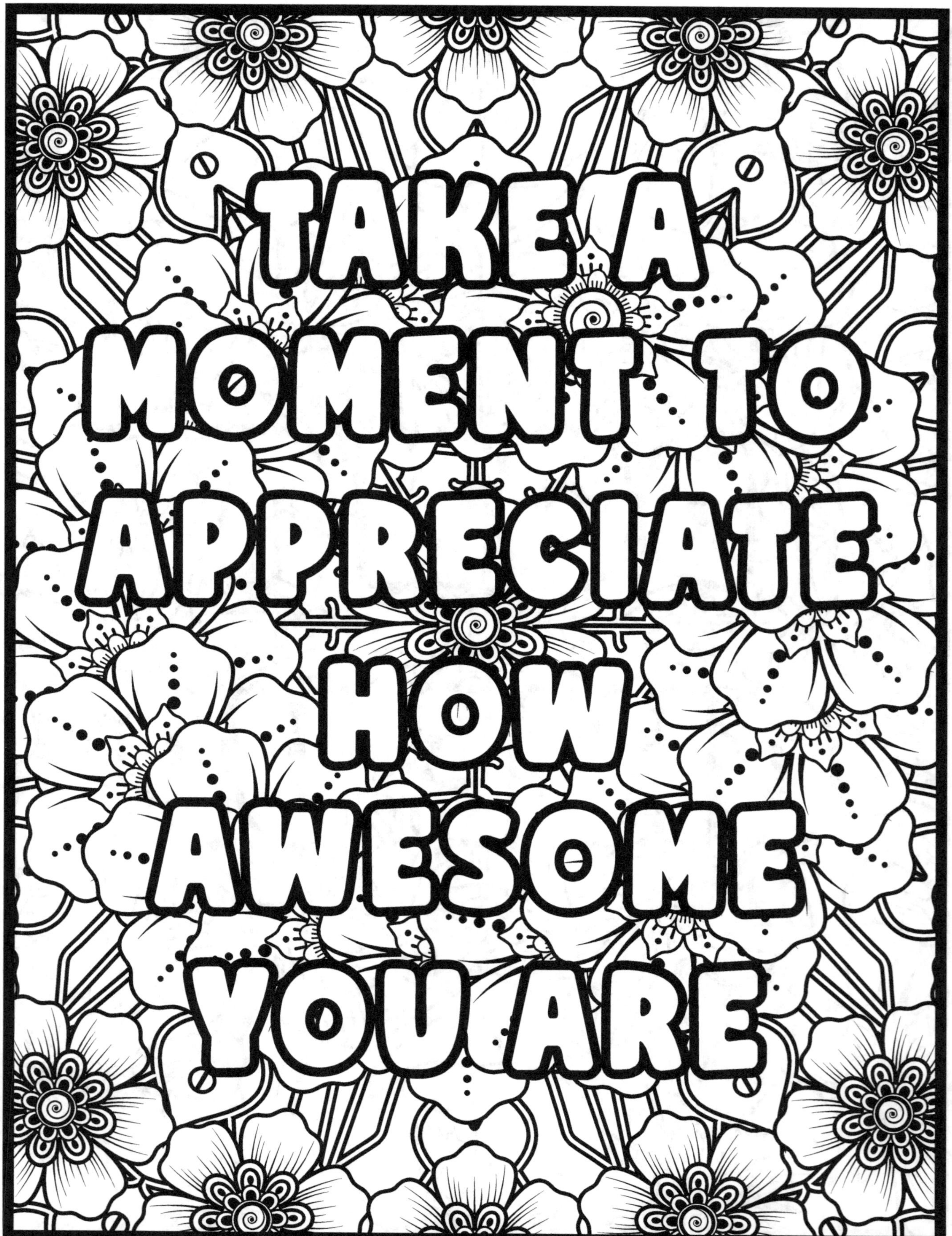
TAKE A
MOMENT TO
APPRECIATE
HOW
AWESOME
YOU ARE

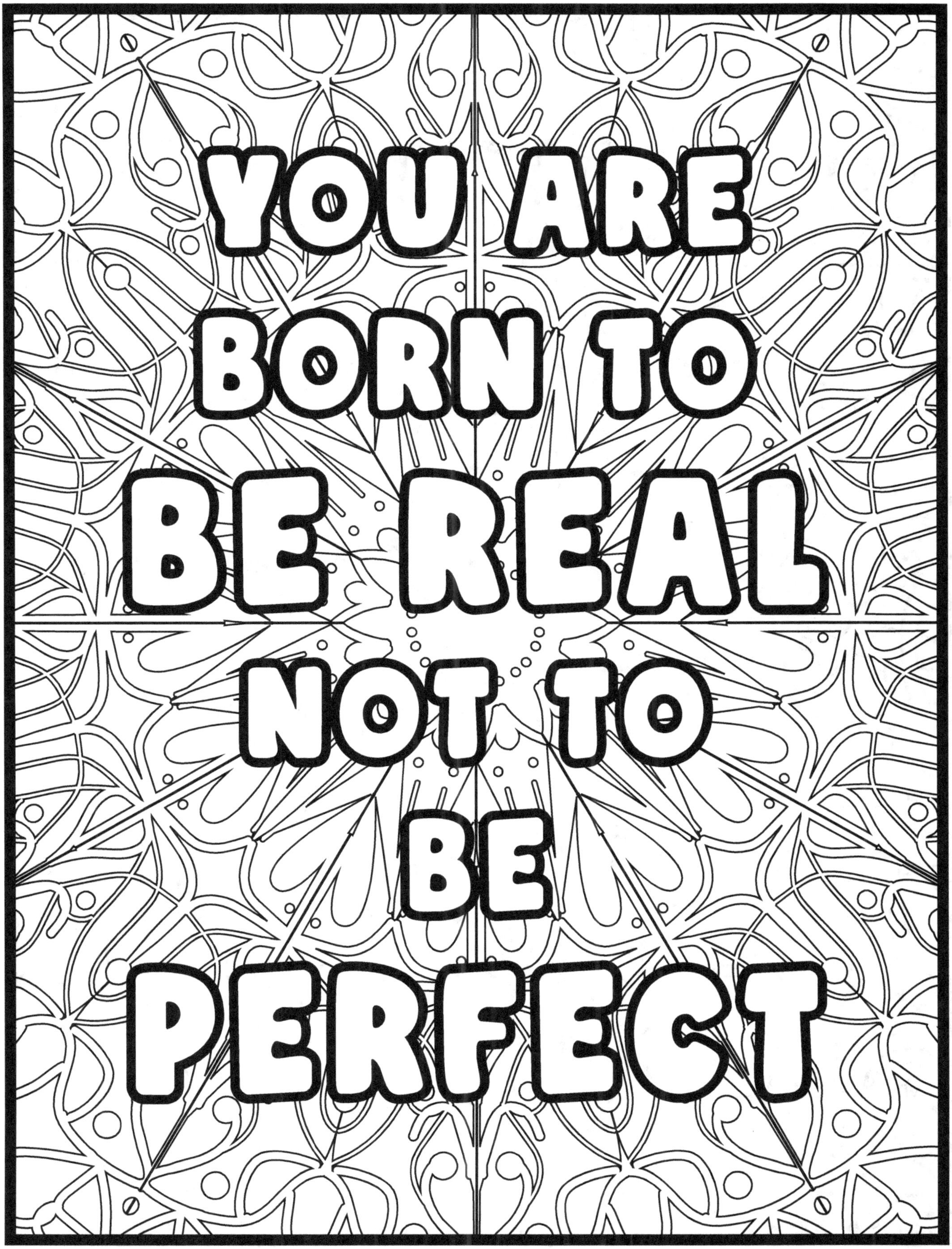
YOU ARE
BORN TO
BE REAL
NOT TO
BE
PERFECT

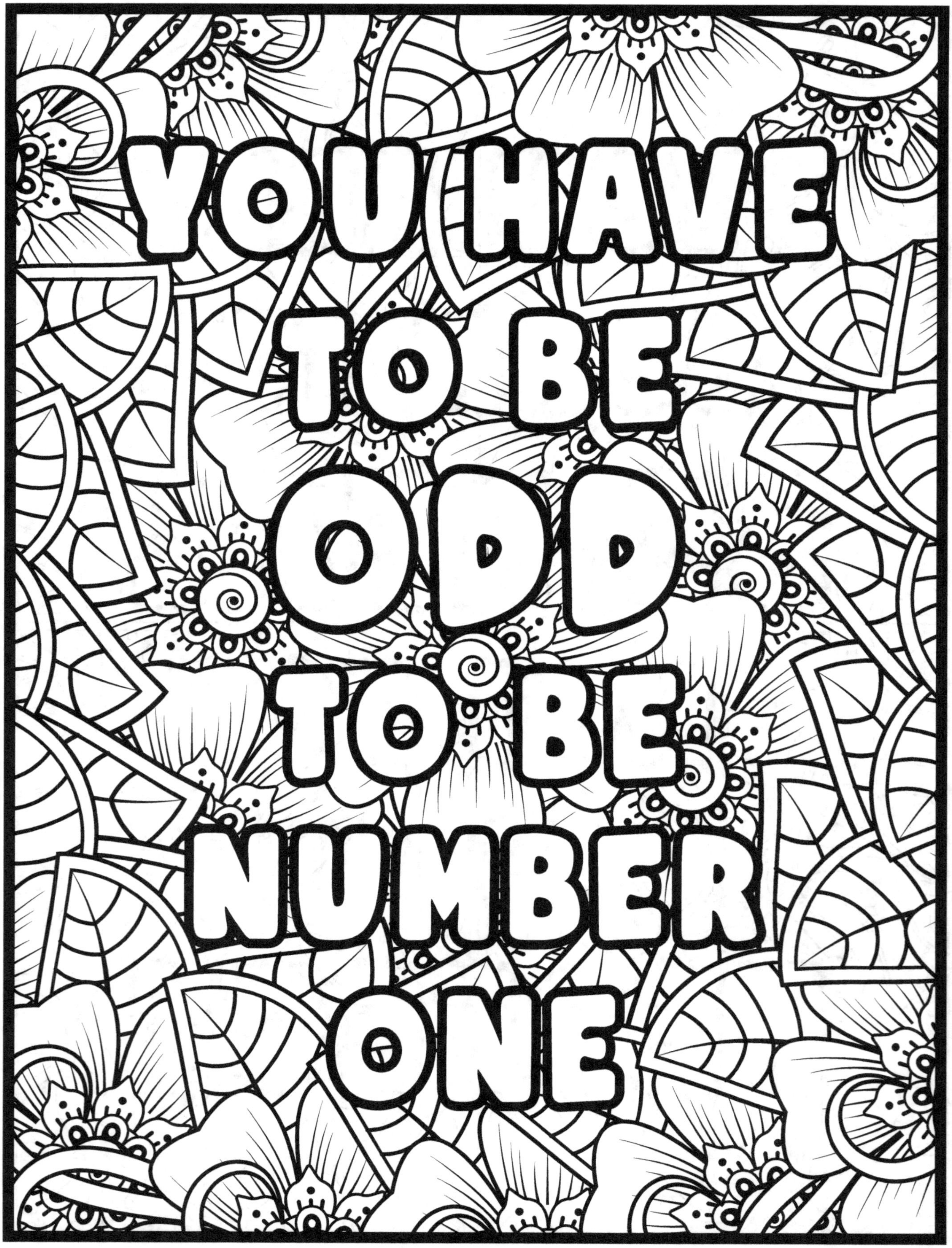
YOU HAVE
TO BE
ODD
TO BE
NUMBER
ONE

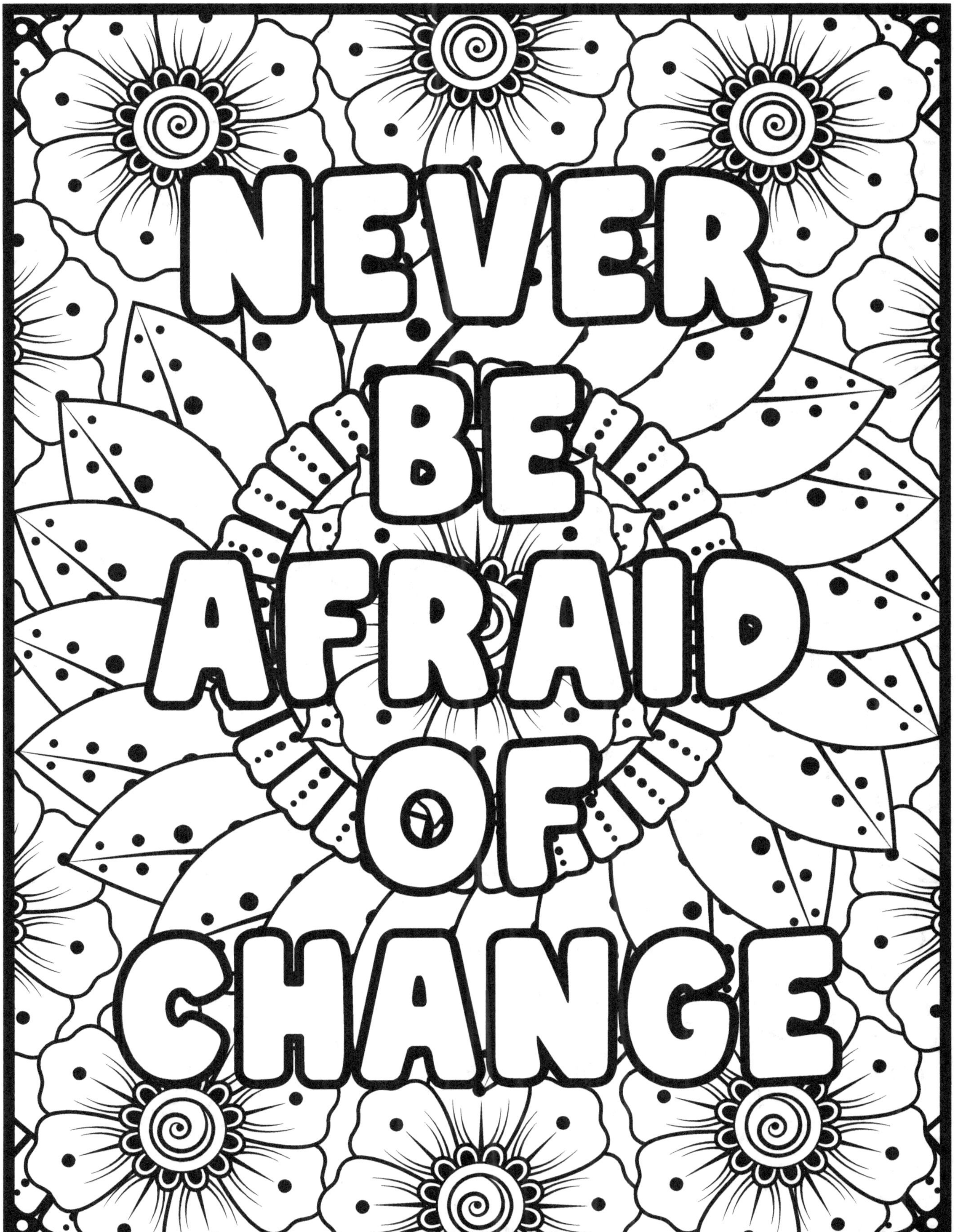
NEVER
BE
AFRAID
OF
CHANGE

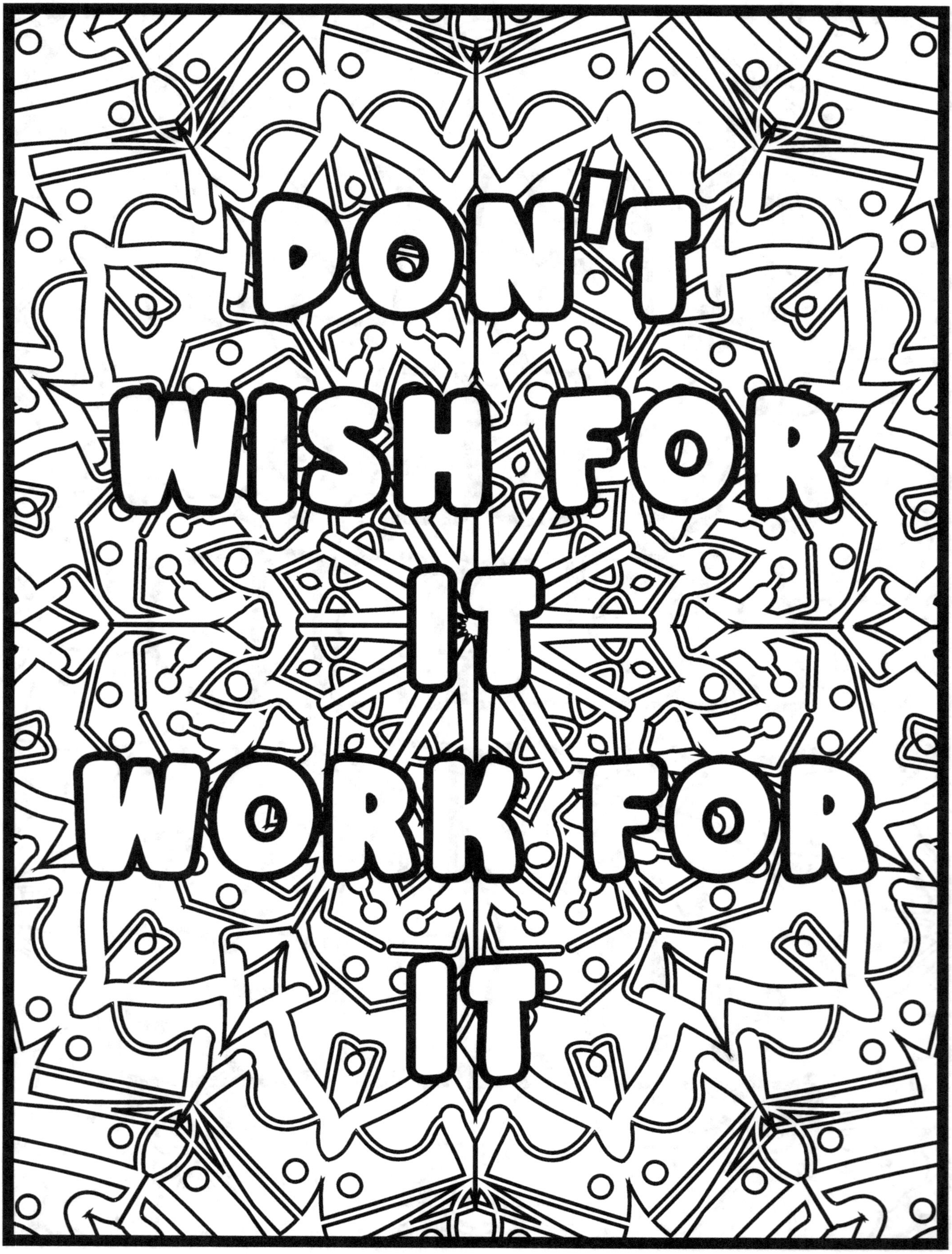
DON'T
WISH FOR
IT
WORK FOR
IT

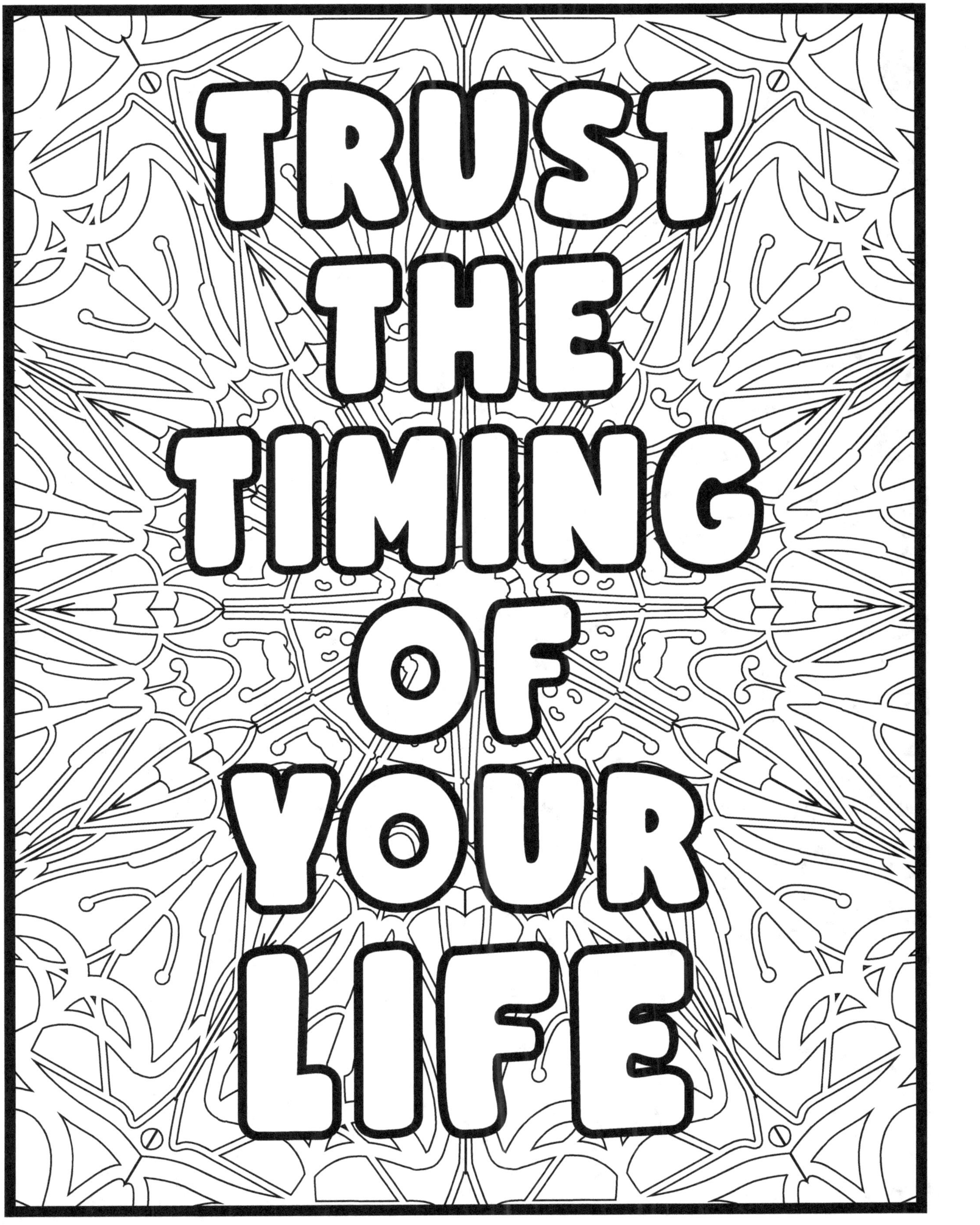
TRUST
THE
TIMING
OF
YOUR
LIFE

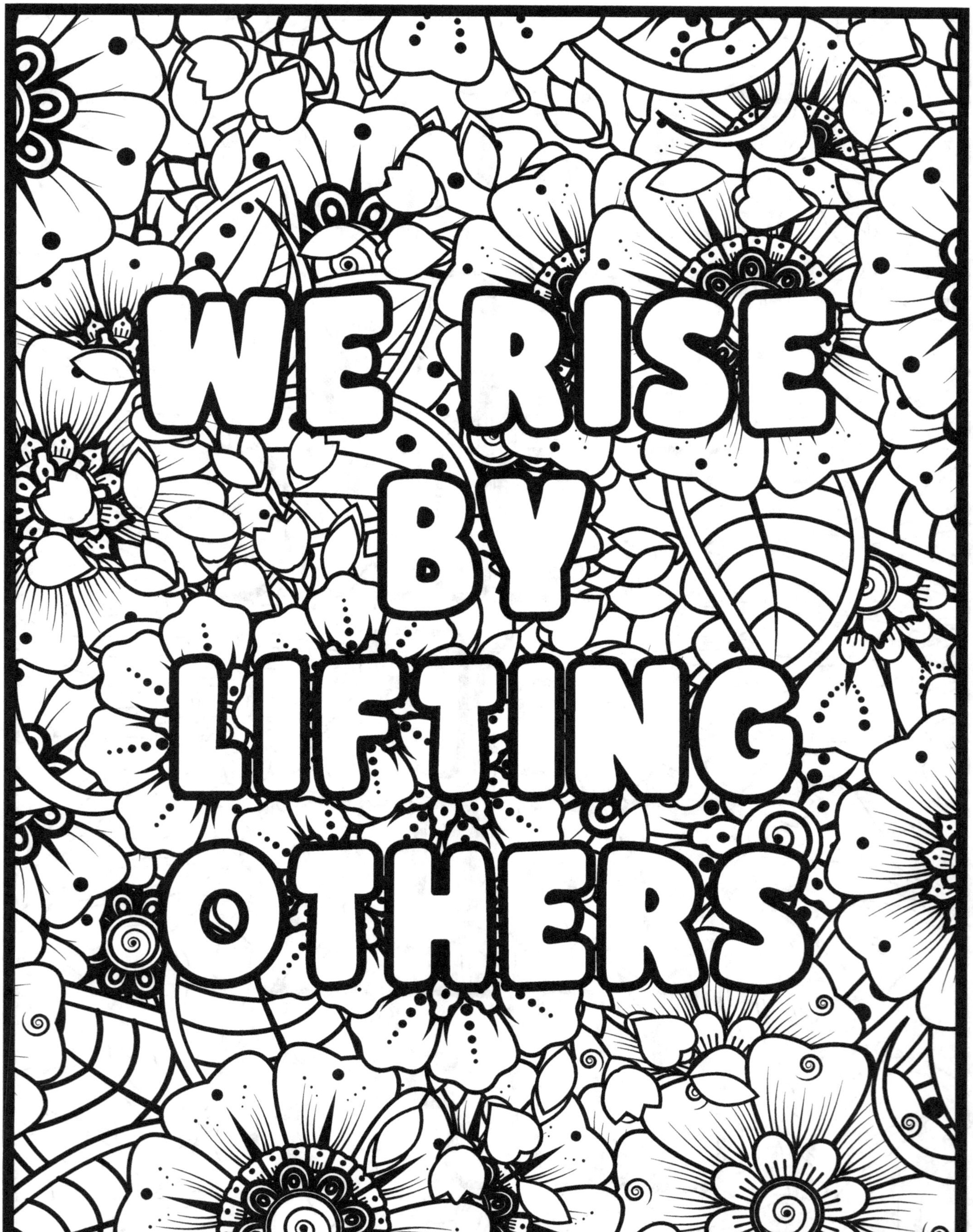
WE RISE
BY
LIFTING
OTHERS

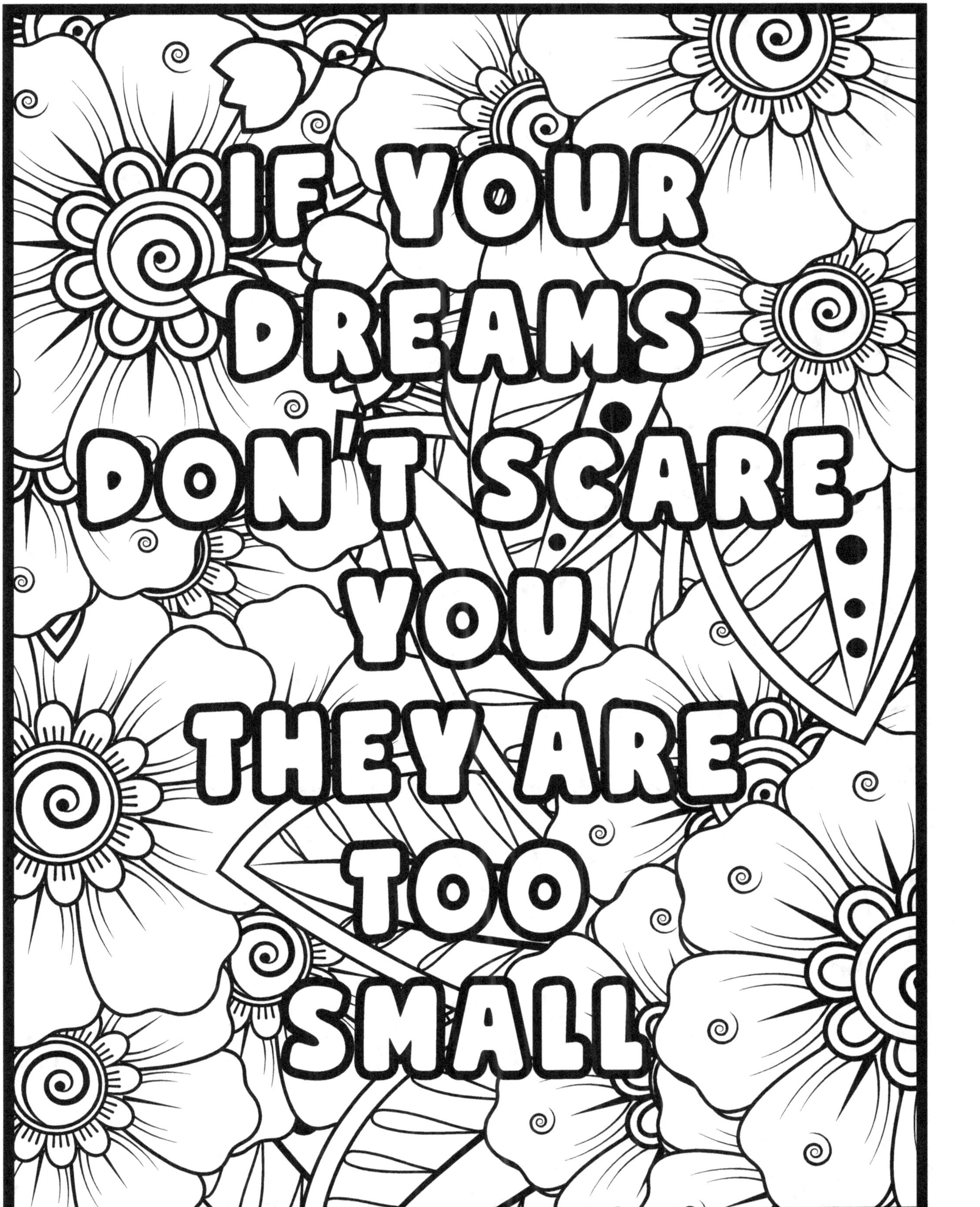
IF YOUR
DREAMS
DON'T SCARE
YOU
THEY ARE
TOO
SMALL

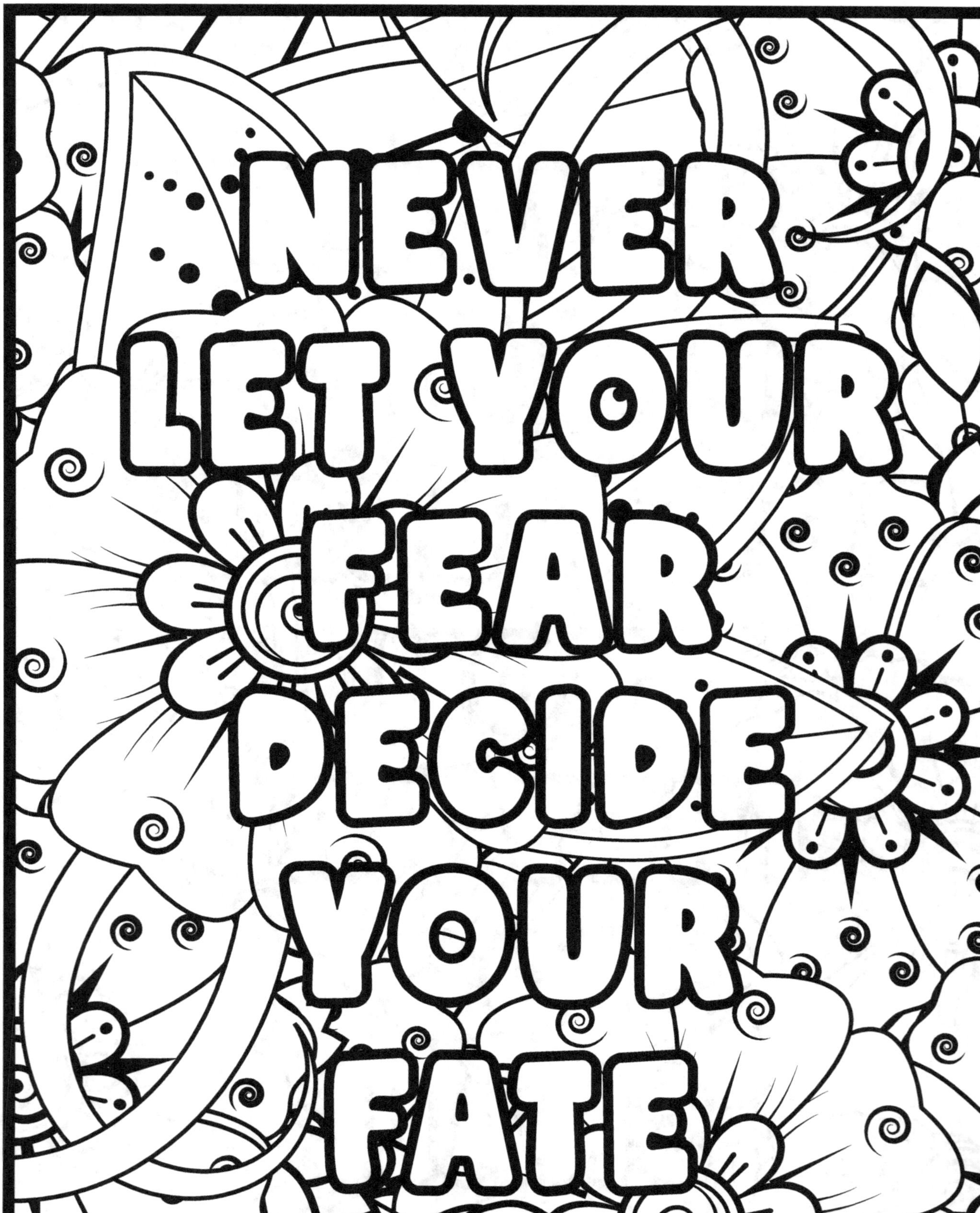
NEVER
LET YOUR
FEAR
DECIDE
YOUR
FATE

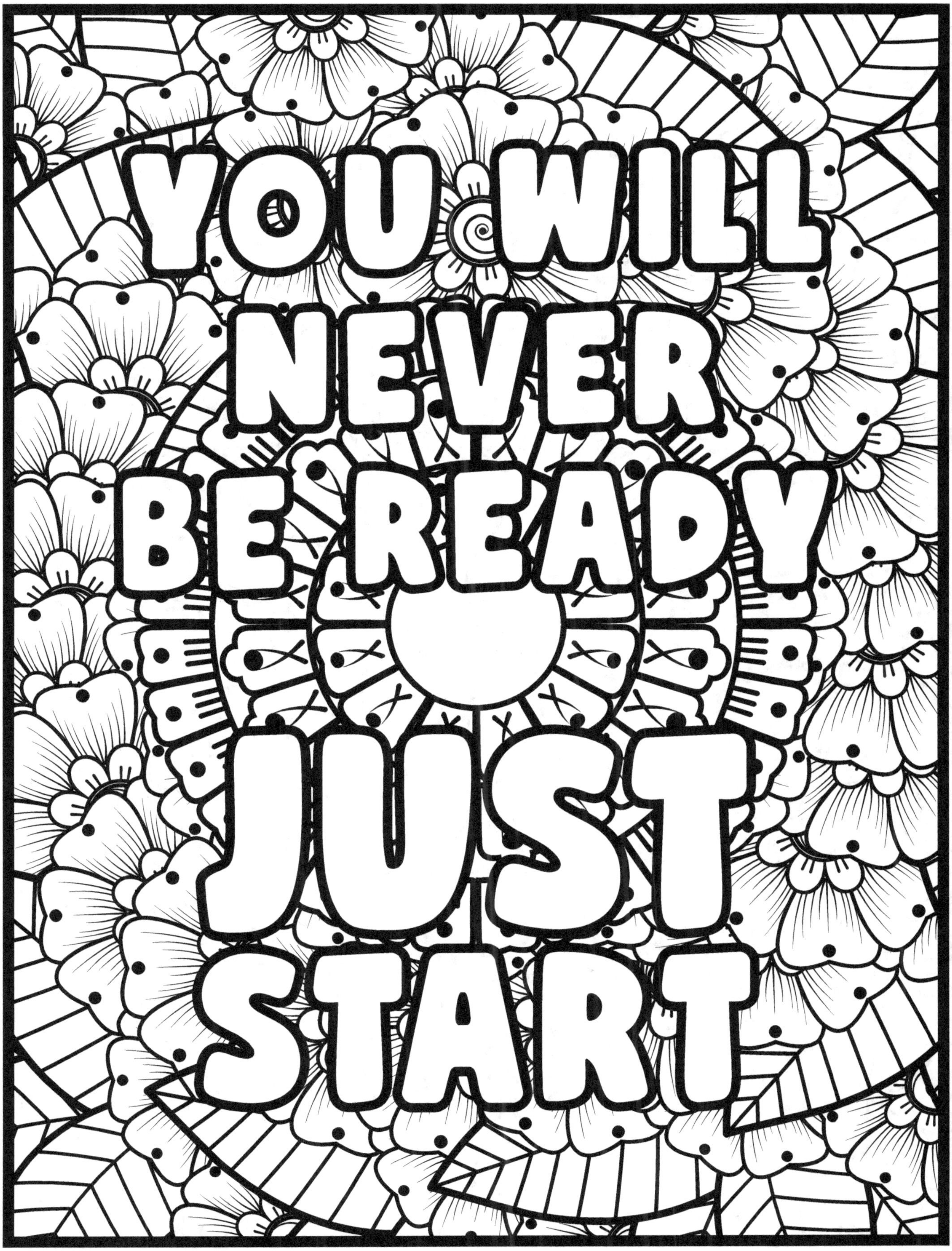
YOU WILL
NEVER
BE READY
JUST
START

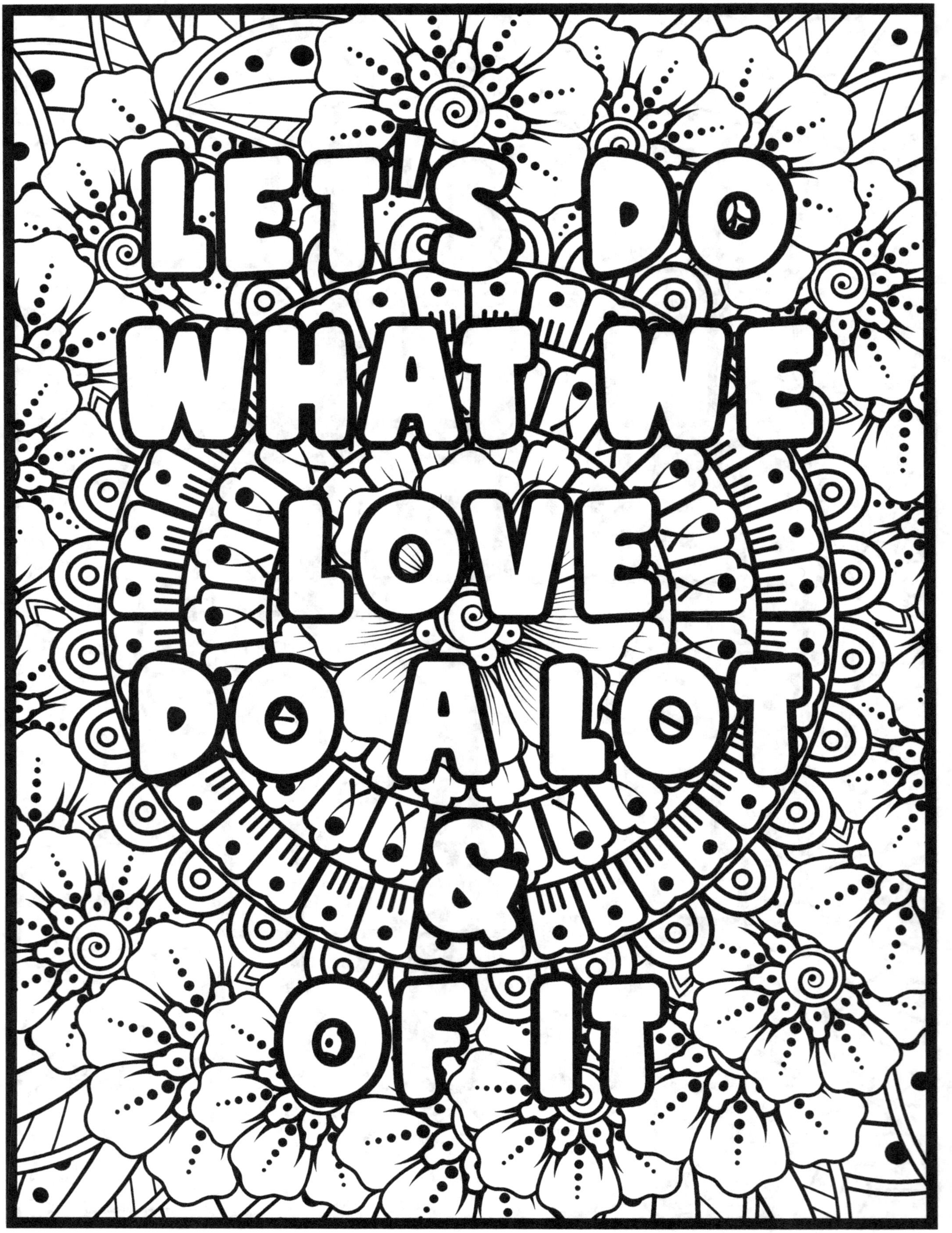
LET'S DO
WHAT WE
LOVE
DO A LOT
&
OF IT

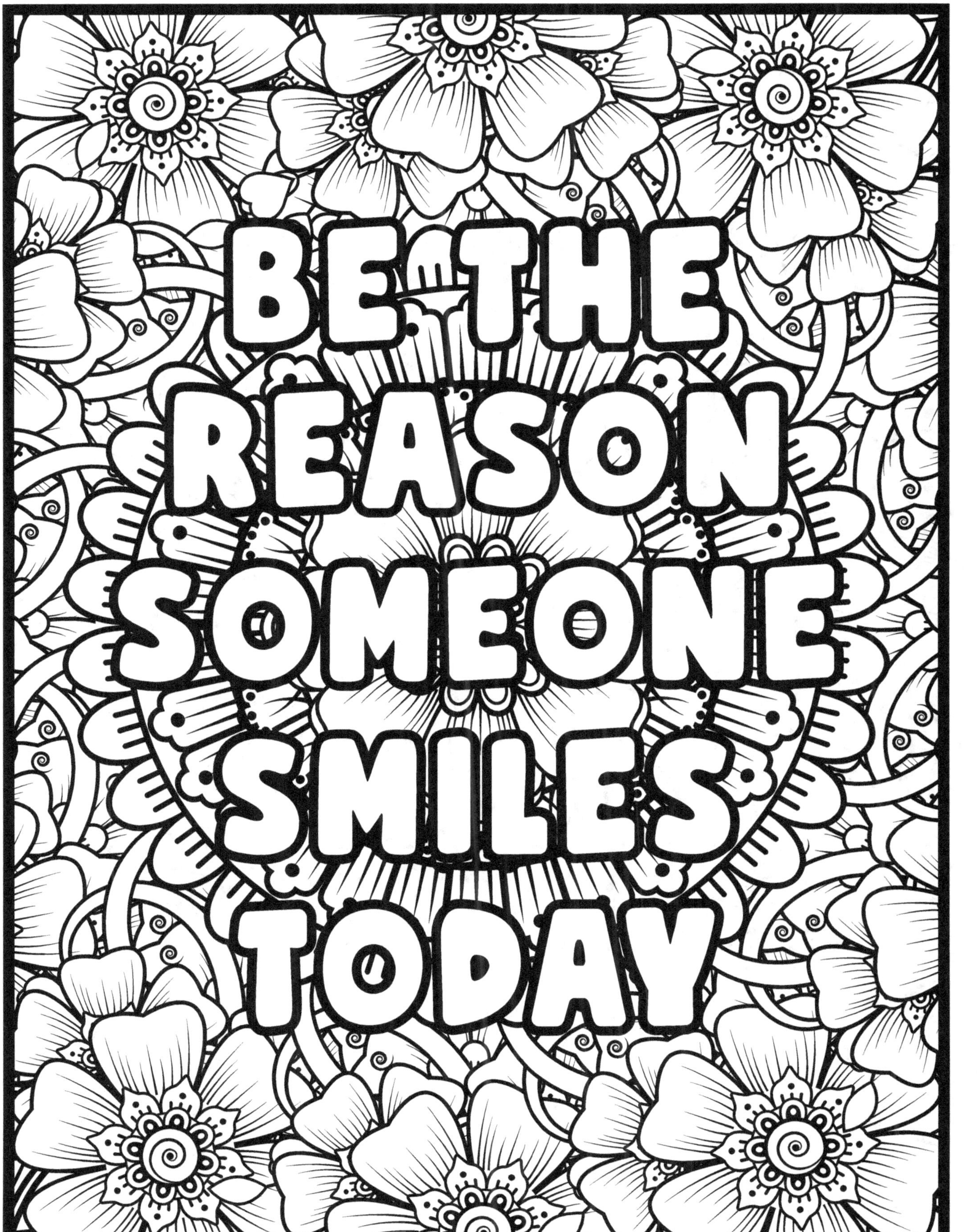
BE THE
REASON
SOMEONE
SMILES
TODAY

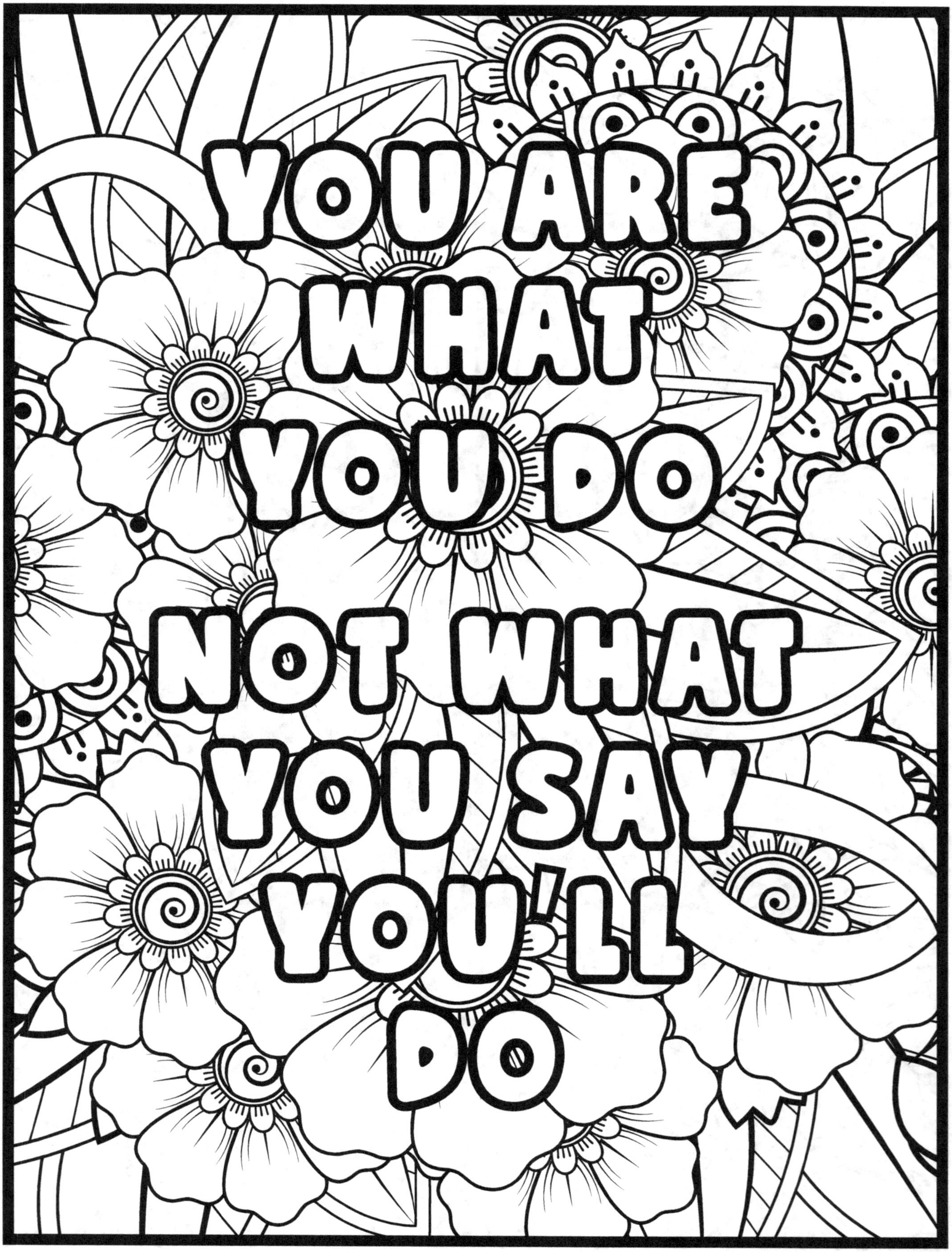
YOU ARE
WHAT
YOU DO
NOT WHAT
YOU SAY
YOU'LL
DO

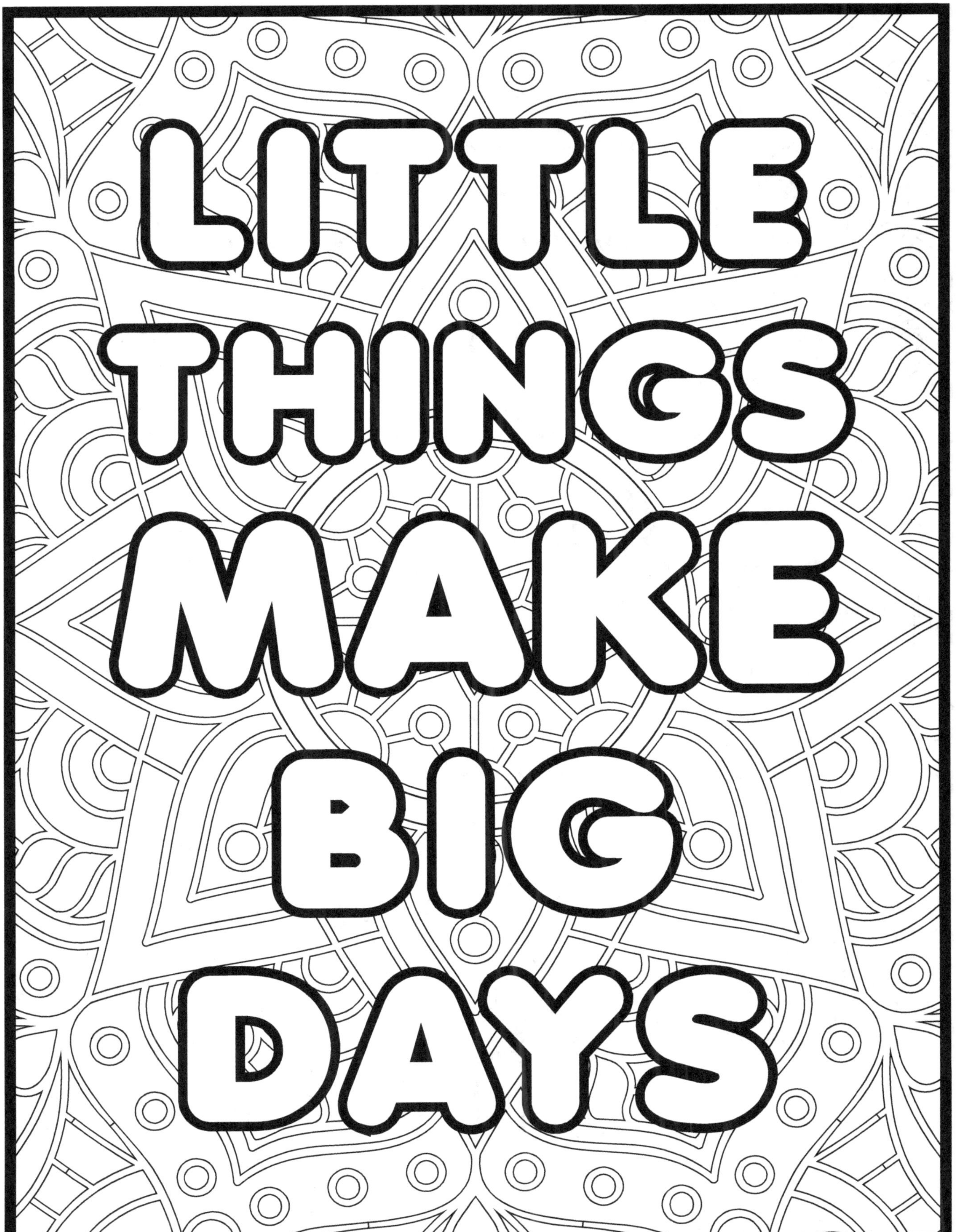
LITTLE
THINGS
MAKE
BIG
DAYS

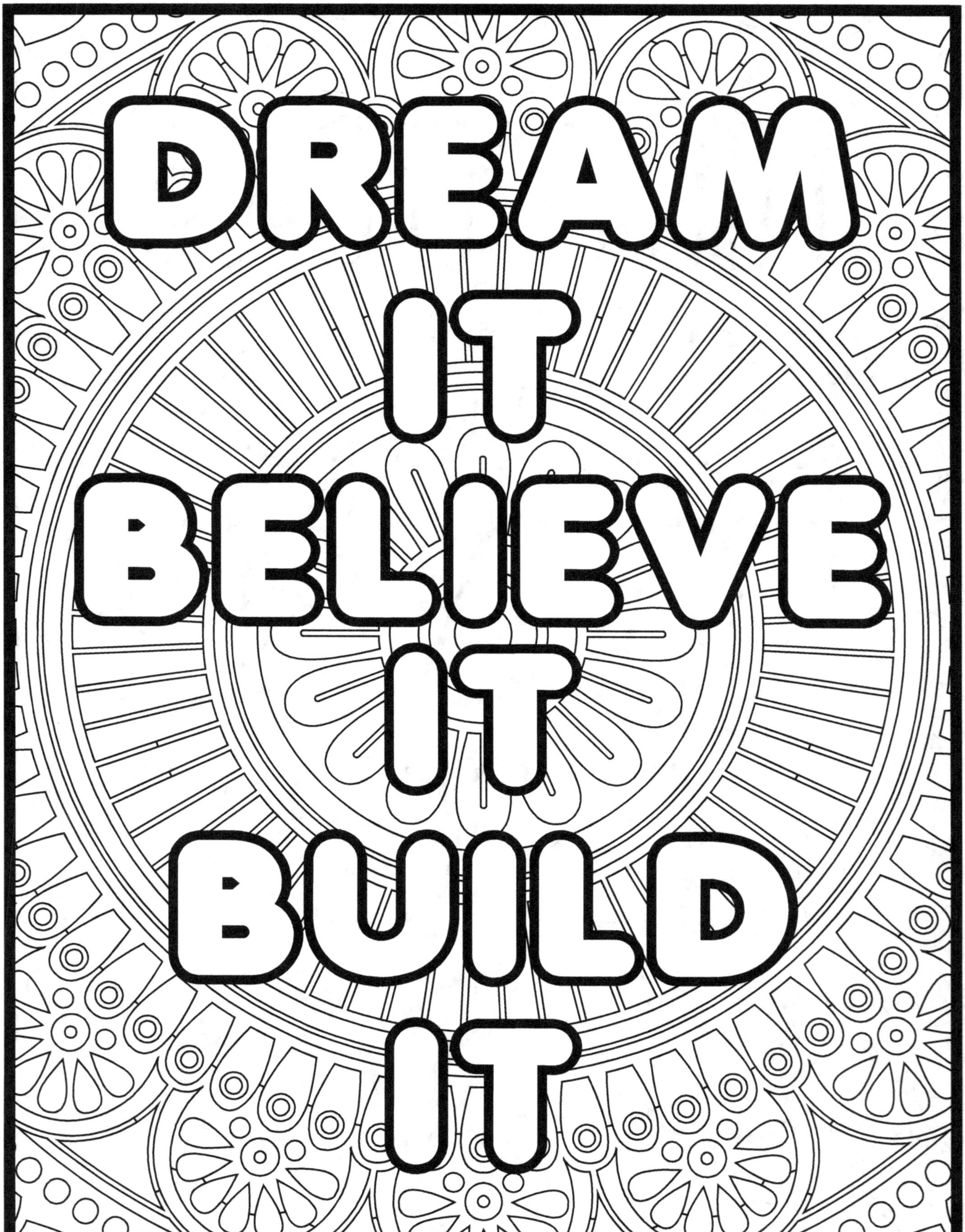
DREAM
IT
BELIEVE
IT
BUILD
IT

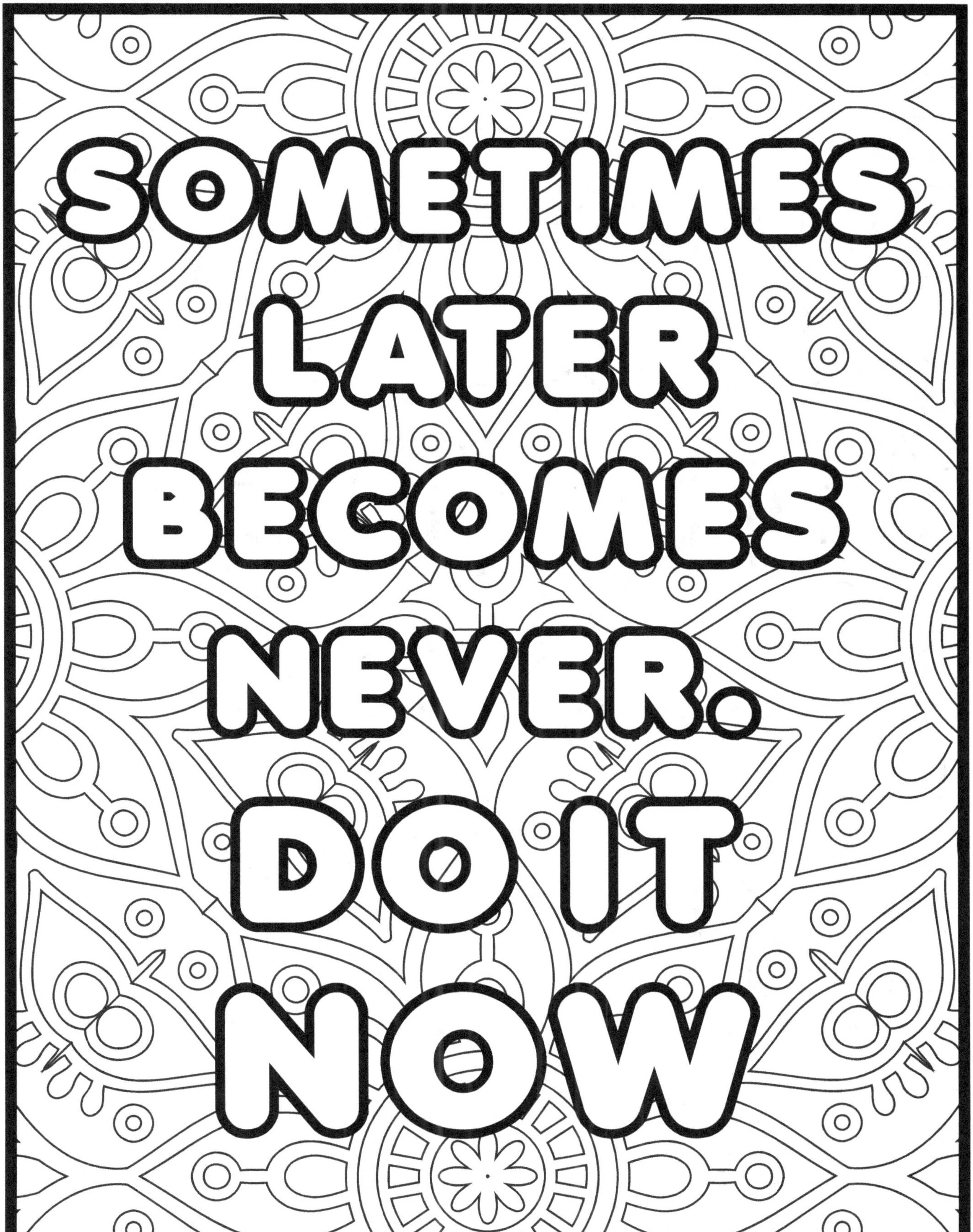
SOMETIMES
LATER
BECOMES
NEVER.
DO IT
NOW

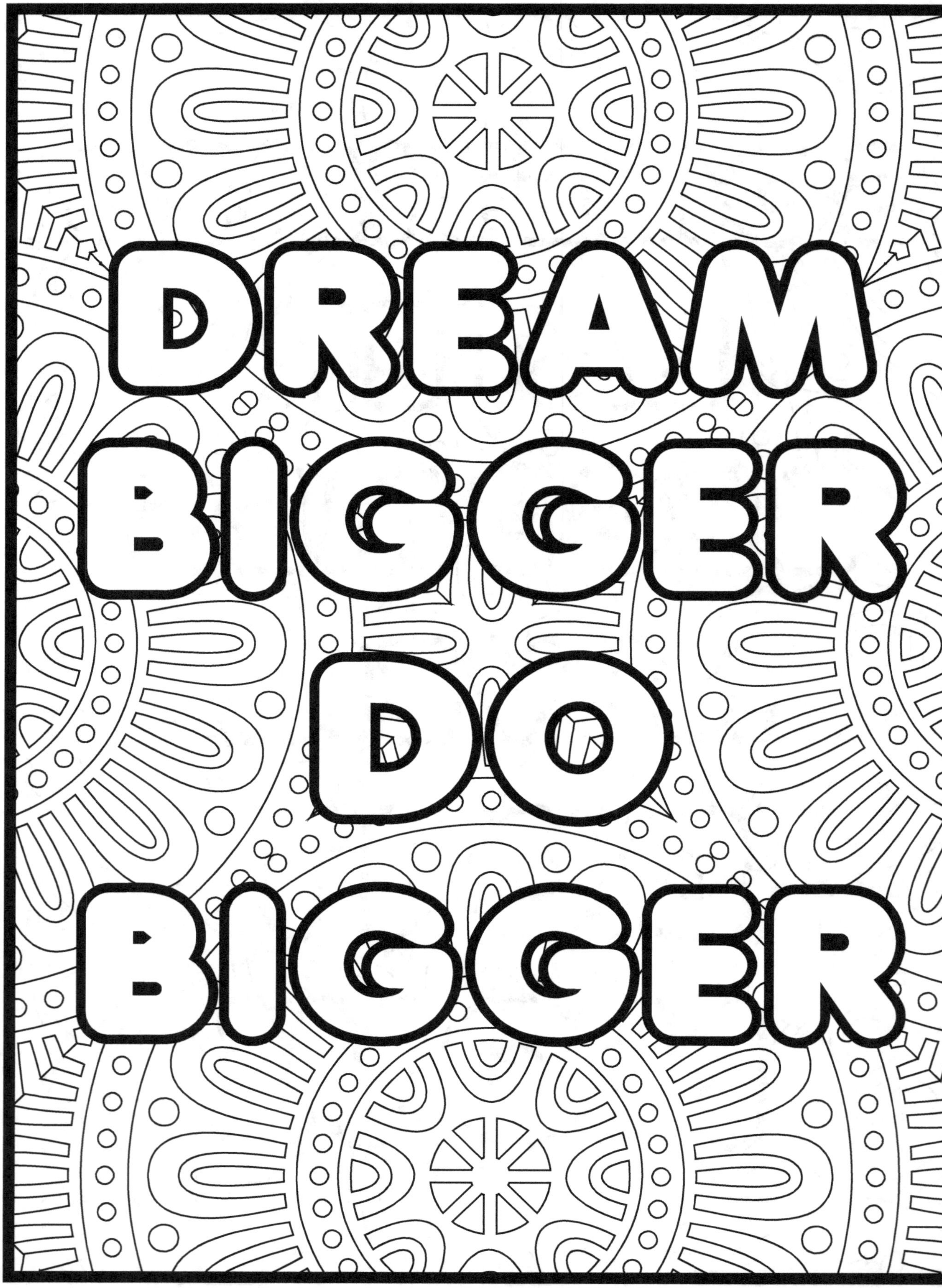
DREAM
BIGGER
DO
BIGGER

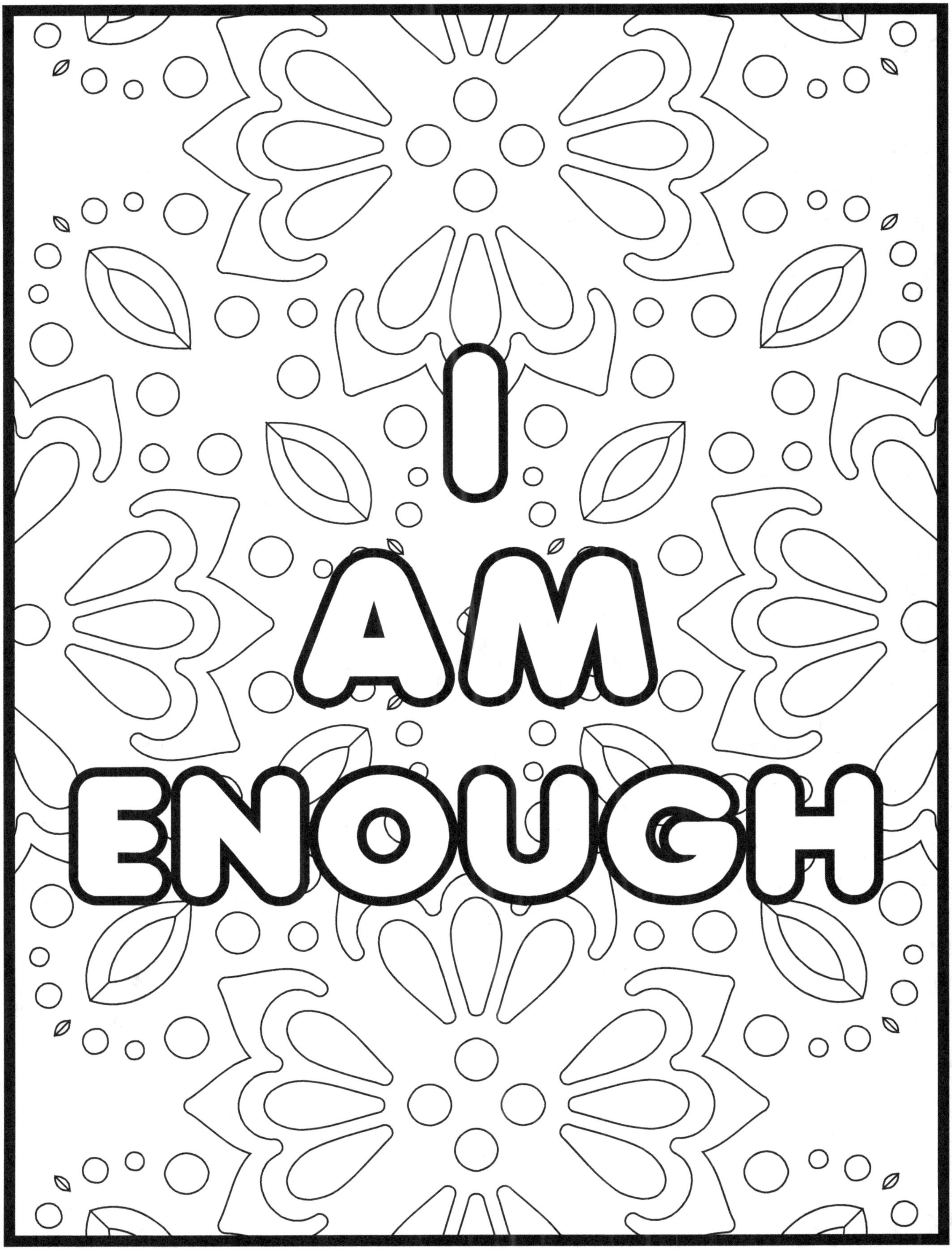
I
AM
ENOUGH

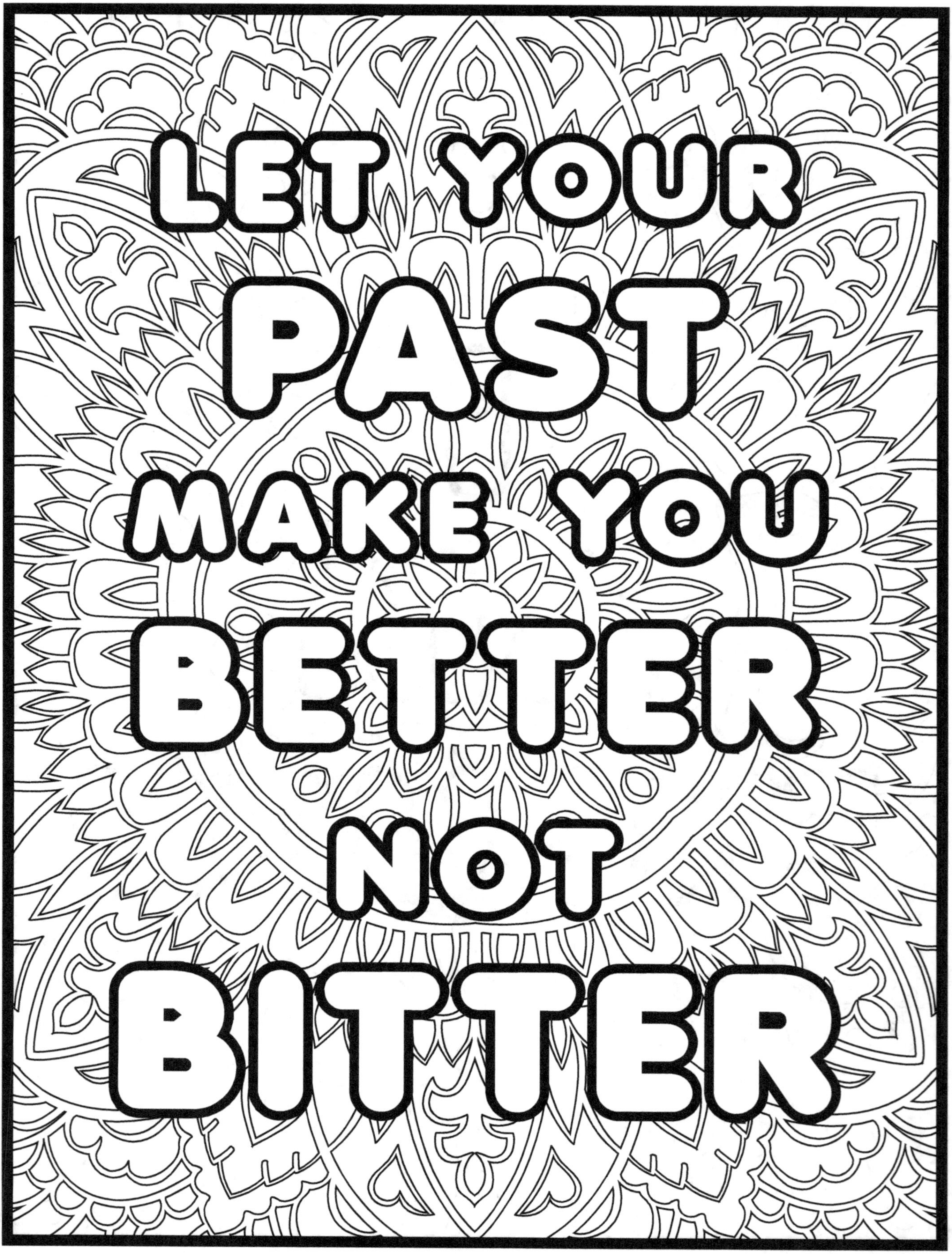
LET YOUR
PAST
MAKE YOU
BETTER
NOT
BITTER

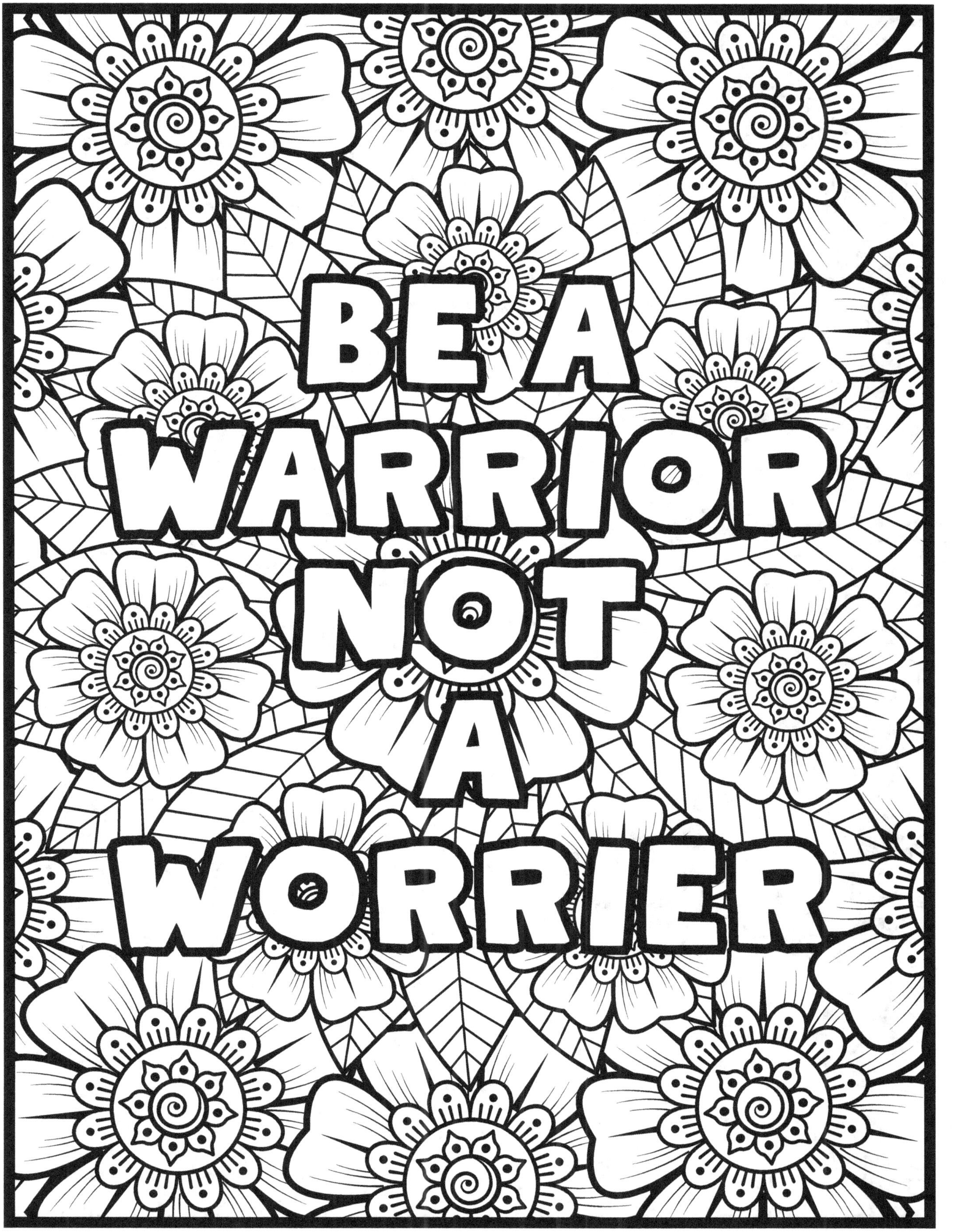
BE A
WARRIOR
NOT
A
WORRIER

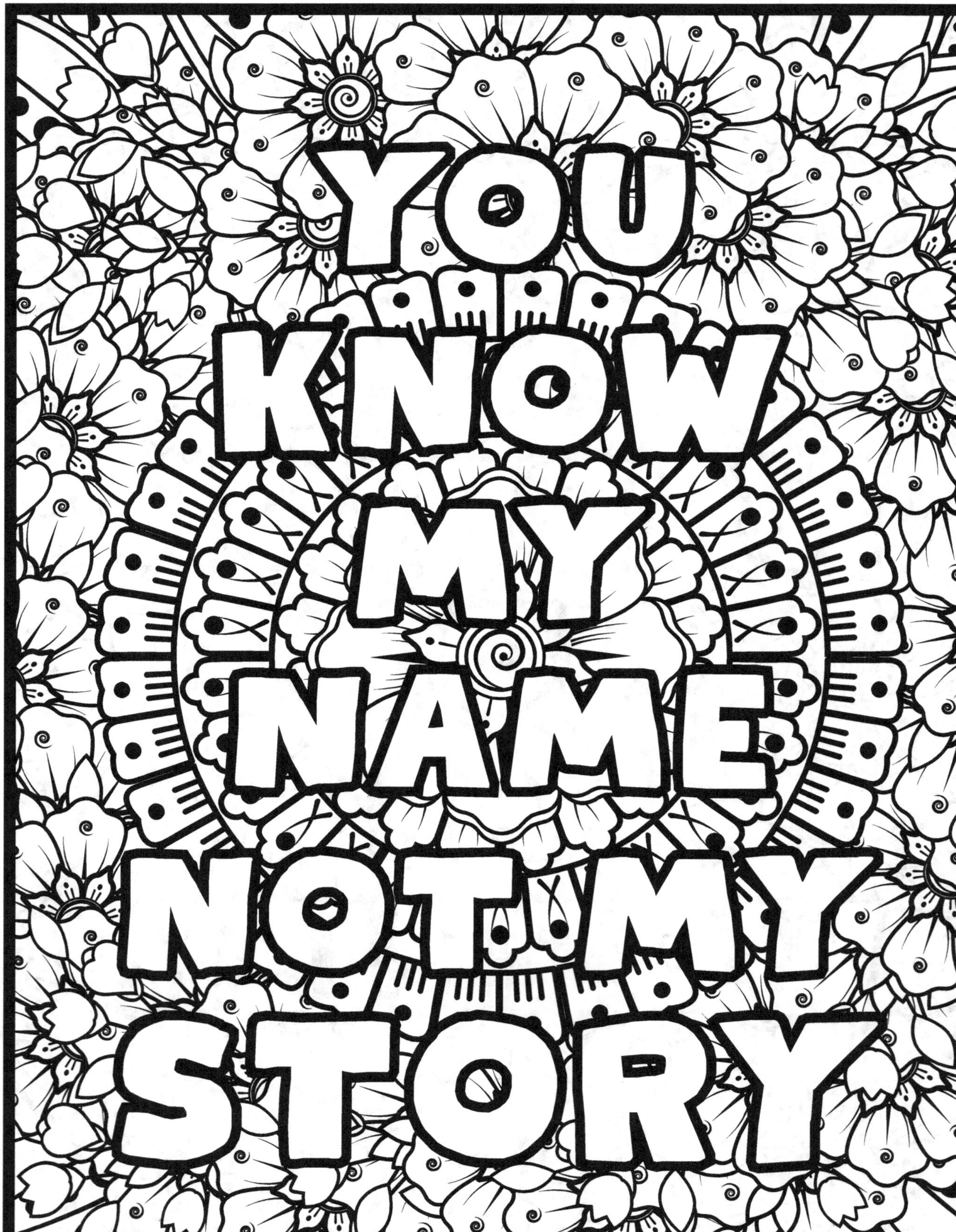
YOU
KNOW
MY
NAME
NOT MY
STORY

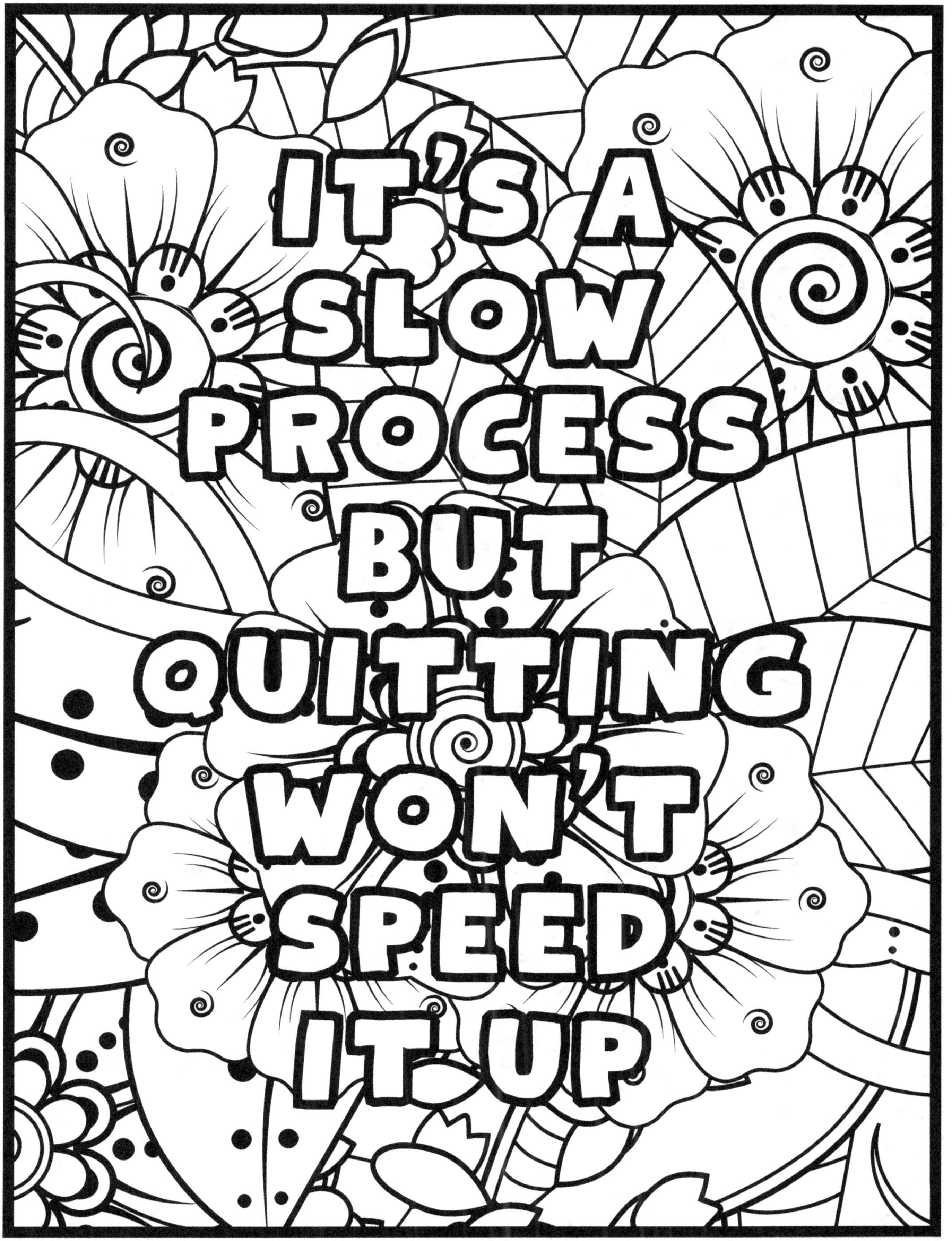
IT'S A
SLOW
PROCESS
BUT
QUITTING
WON'T
SPEED
IT UP

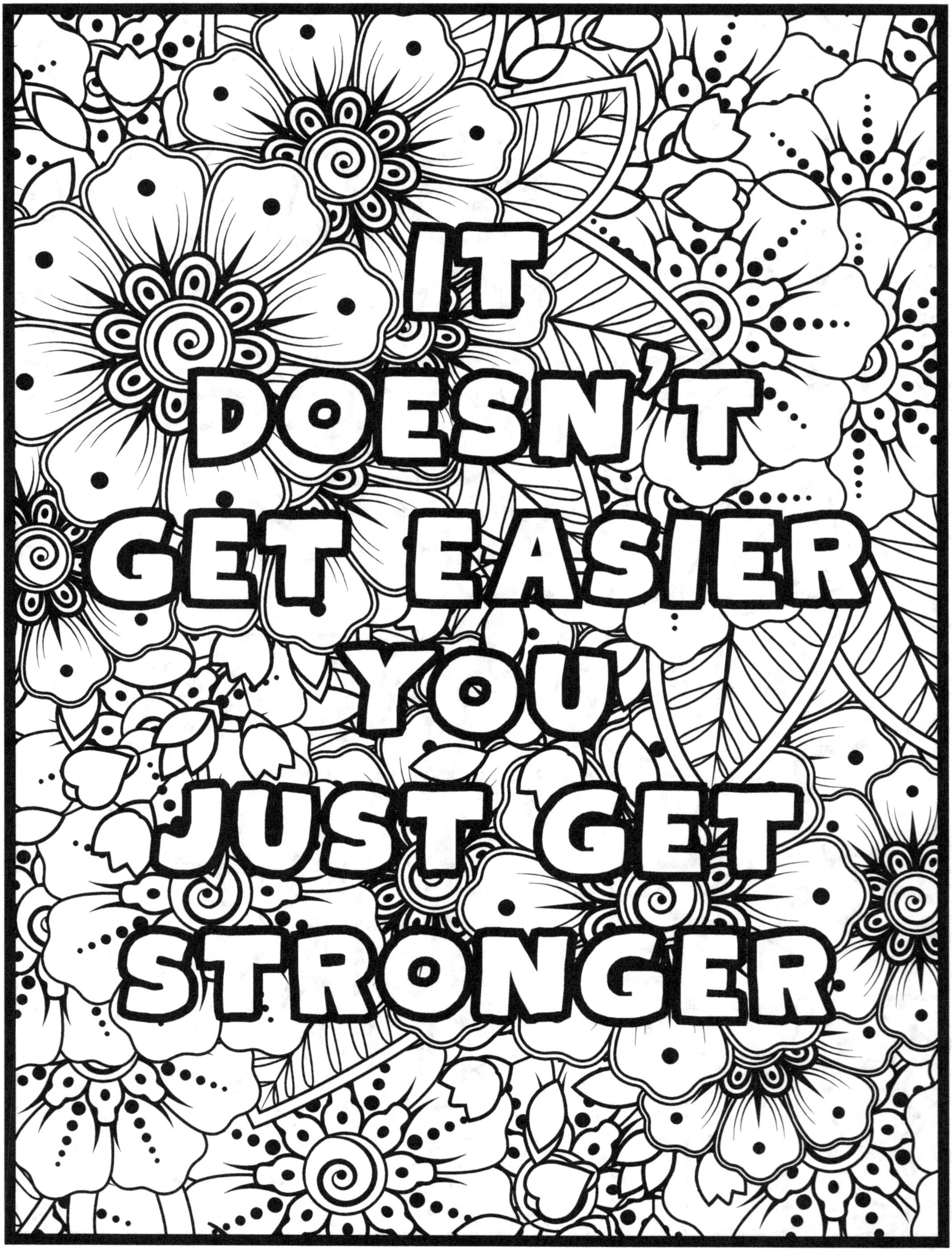
IT
DOESN'T
GET EASIER
YOU
JUST GET
STRONGER

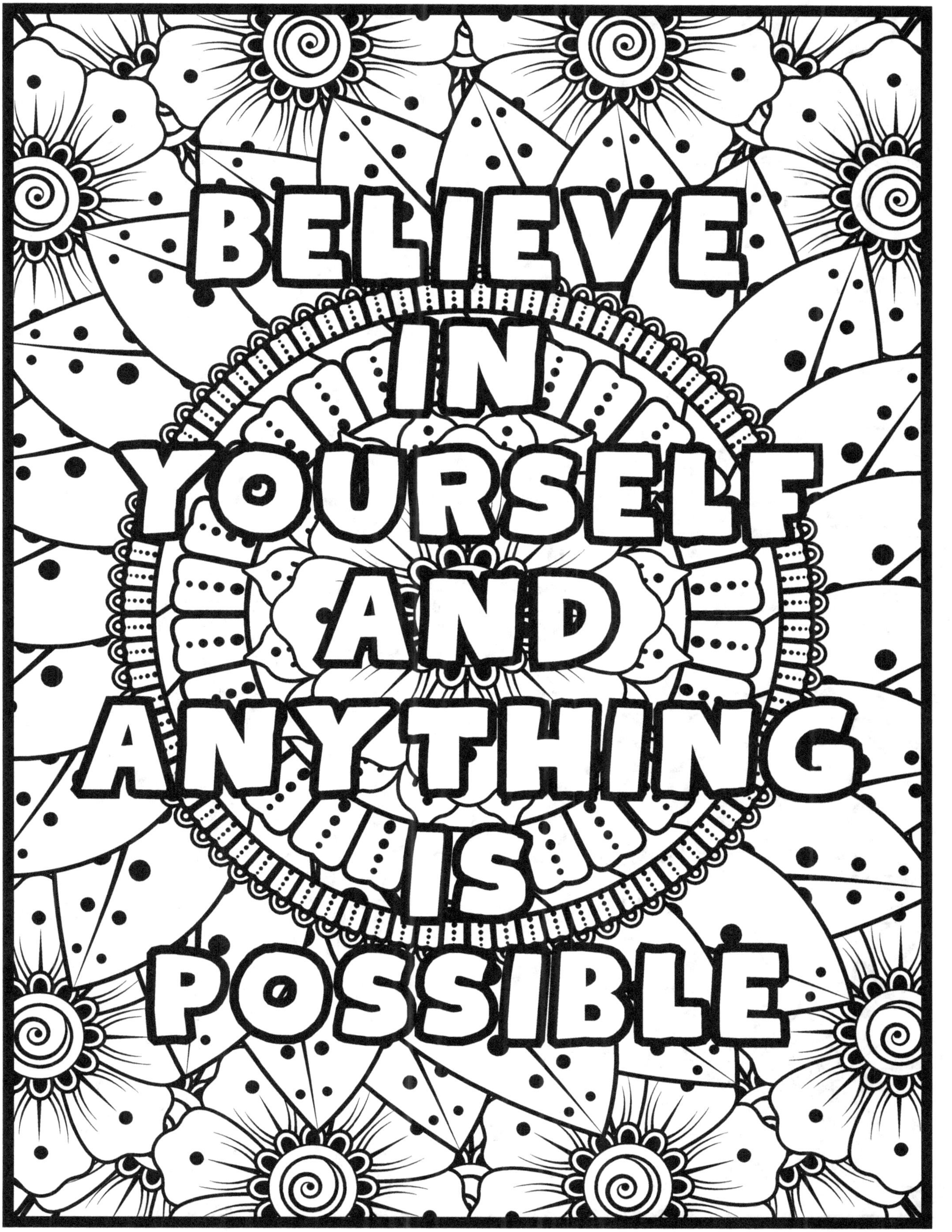
BELIEVE
IN
YOURSELF
AND
ANYTHING
IS
POSSIBLE

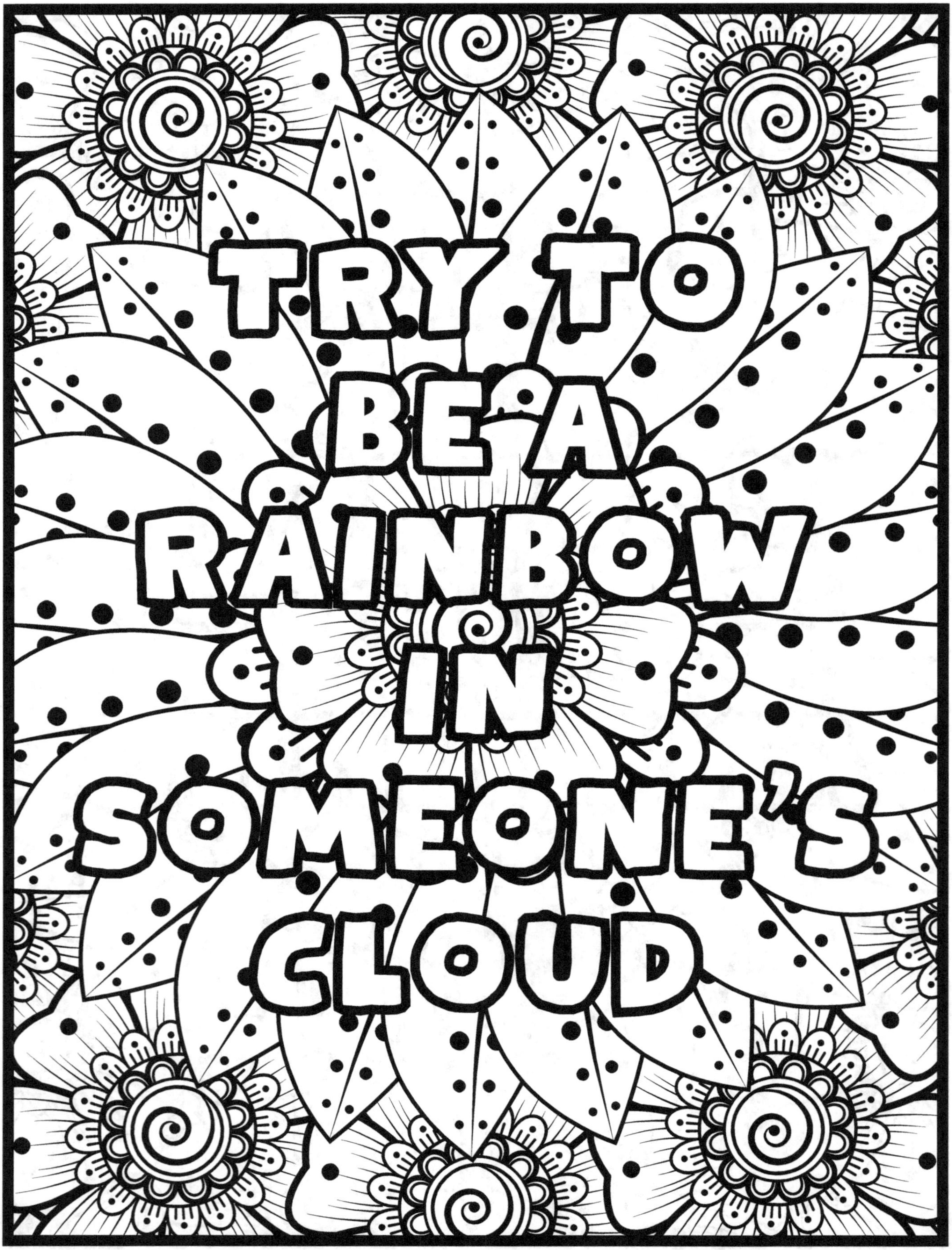
TRY TO
BE A
RAINBOW
IN
SOMEONE'S
CLOUD

EVERYTHING
YOU DO
NOW
IS
FOR
YOUR
FUTURE

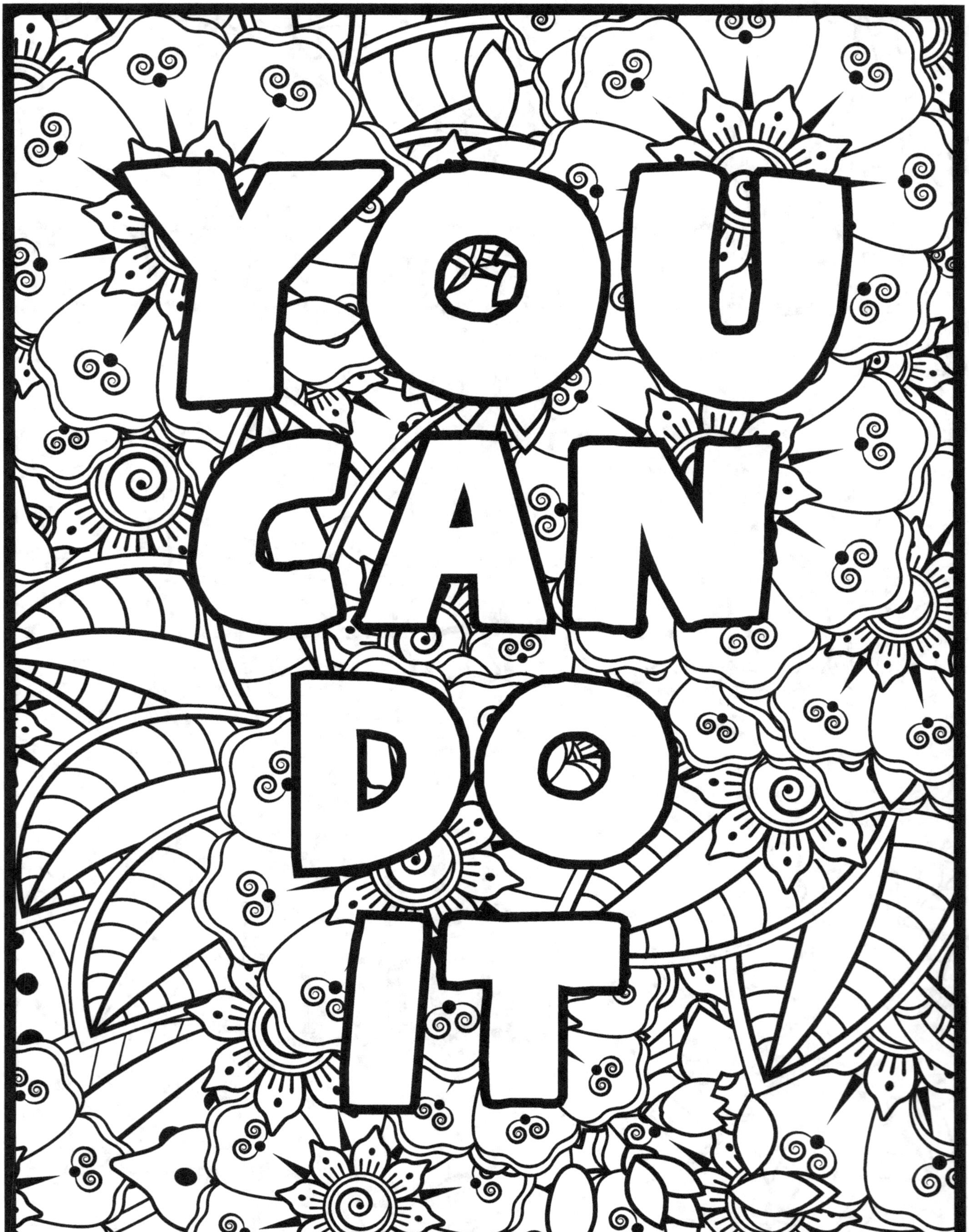
YOU
CAN
DO
IT

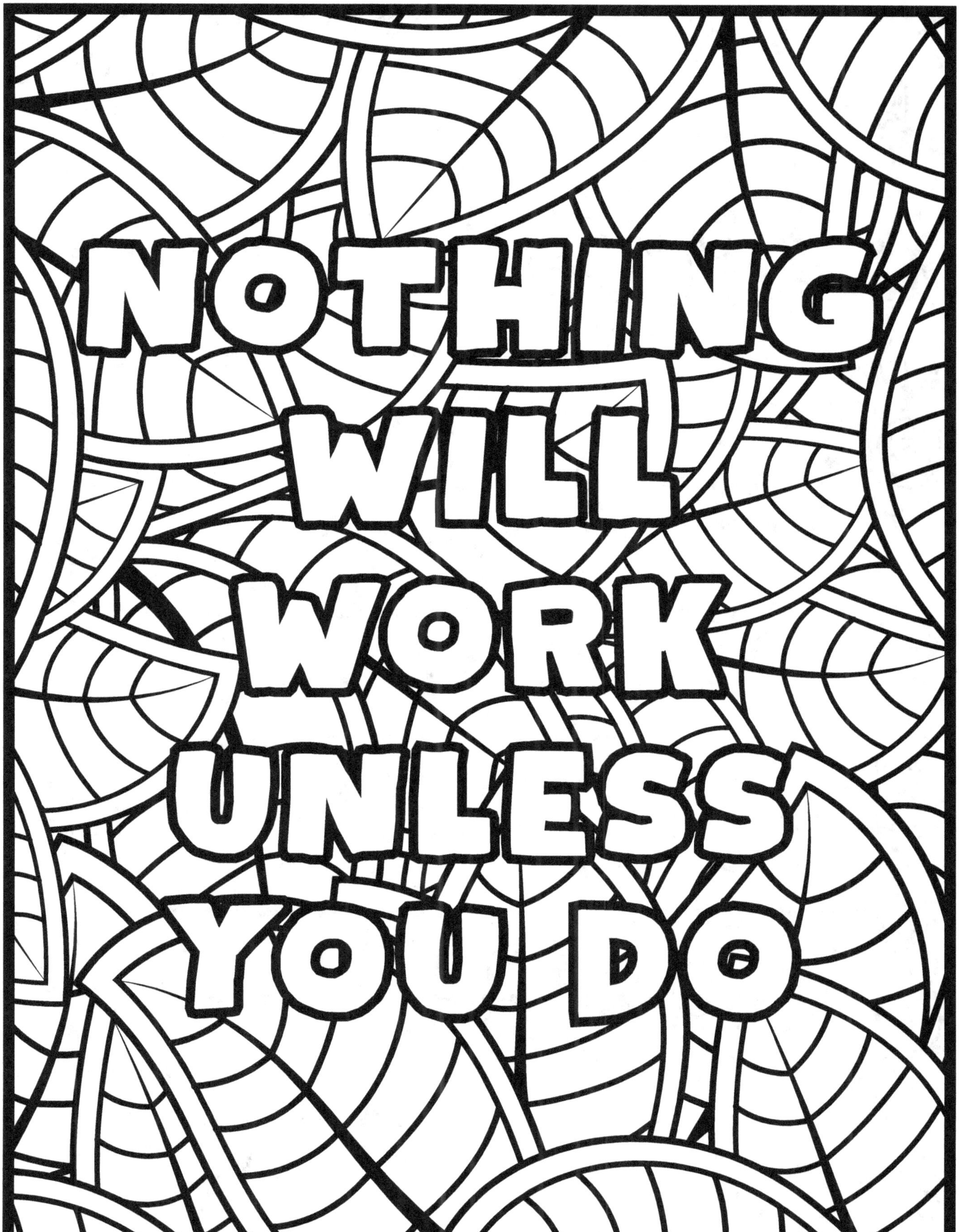
NOTHING
WILL
WORK
UNLESS
YOU DO

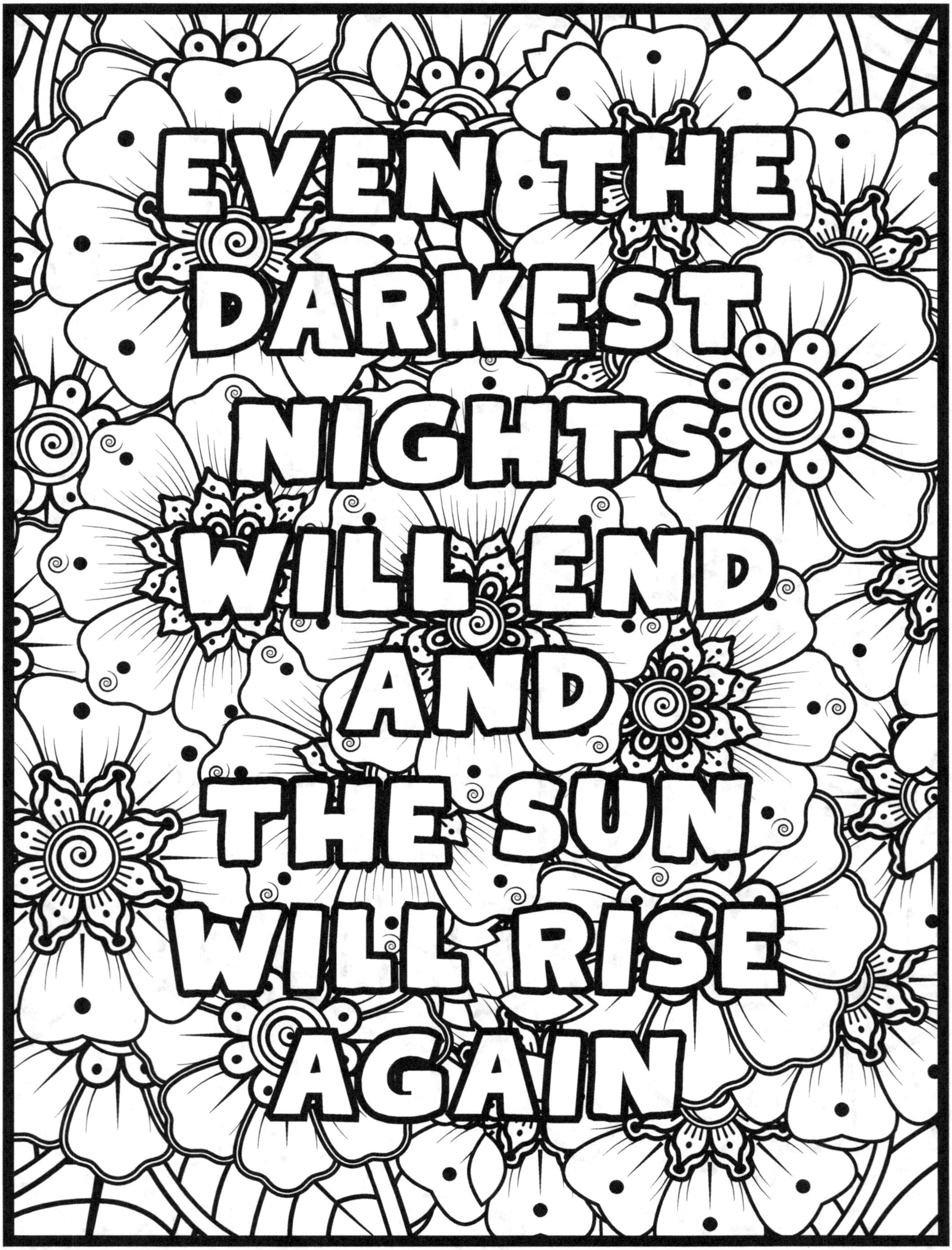
EVEN THE
DARKEST
NIGHTS
WILL END
AND
THE SUN
WILL RISE
AGAIN

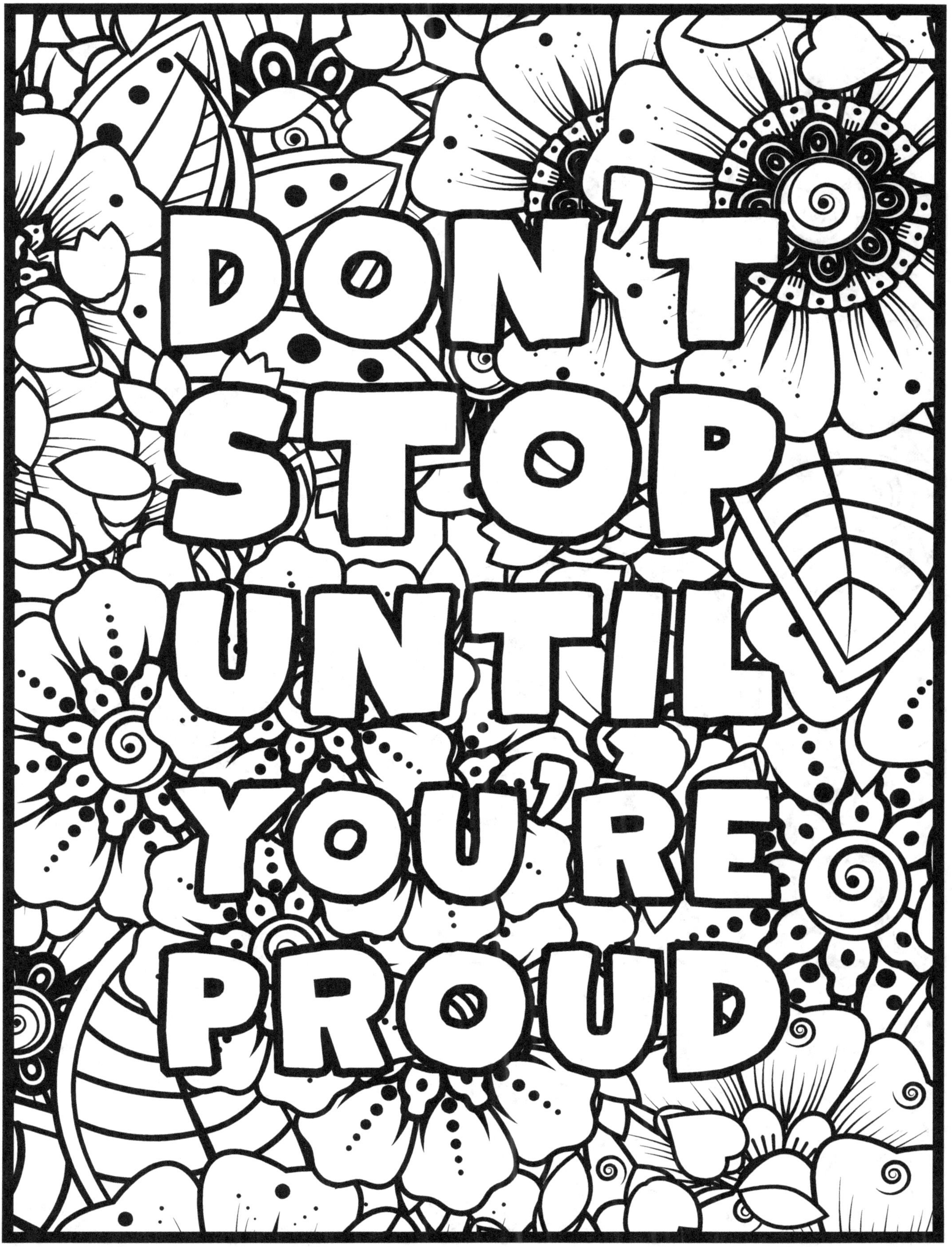
DON'T
STOP
UNTIL
YOU'RE
PROUD

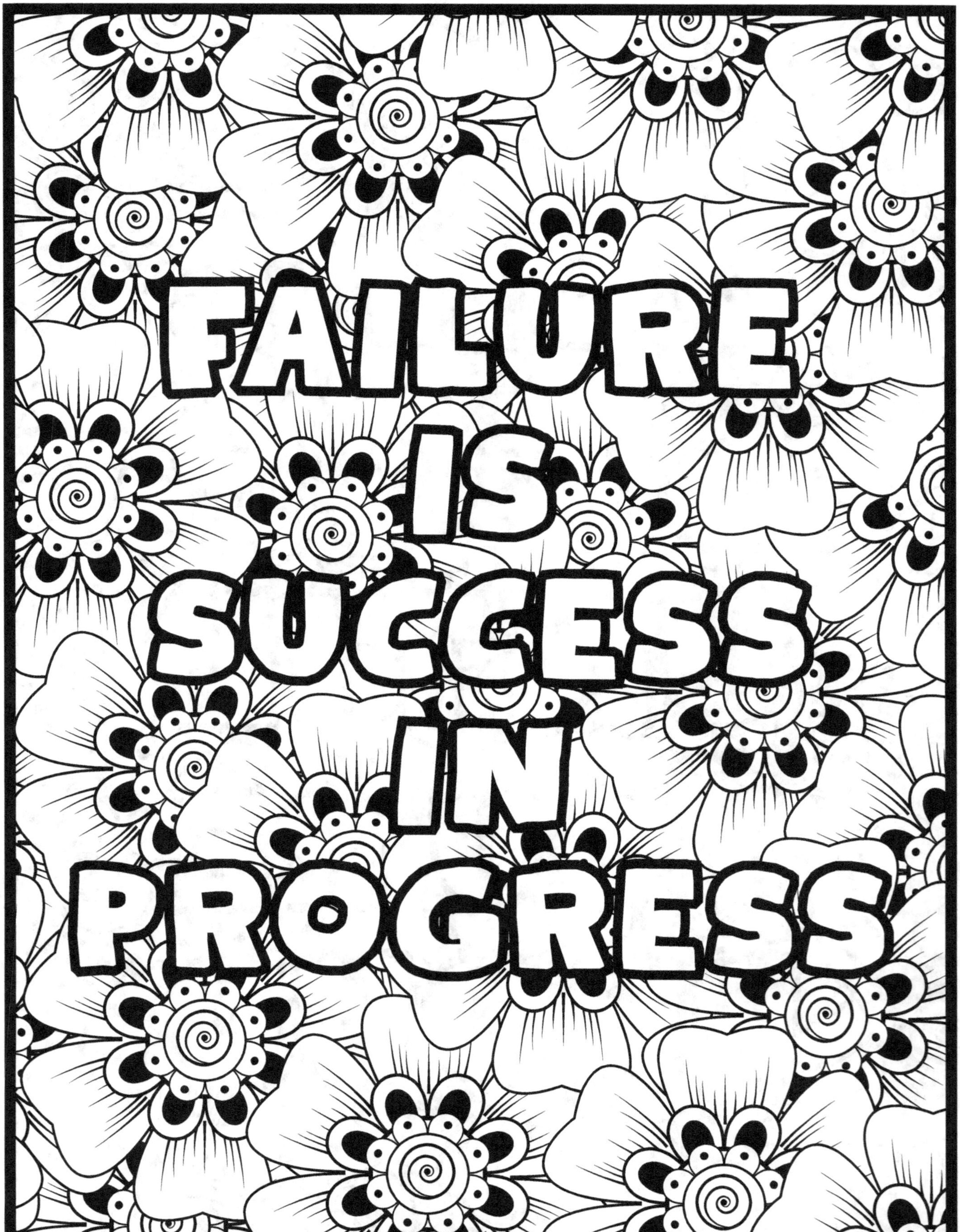
FAILURE
IS
SUCCESS
IN
PROGRESS

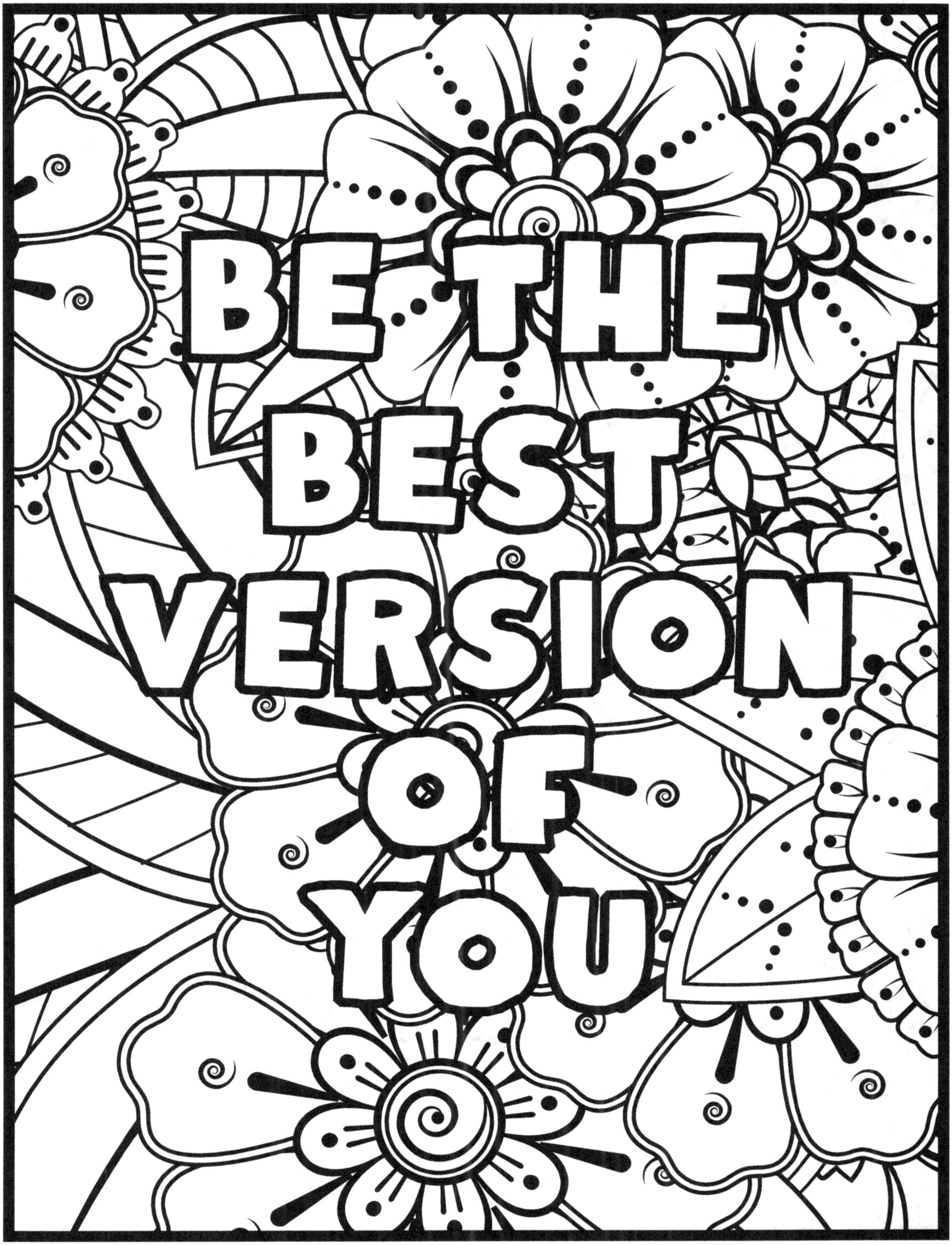
BE THE
BEST
VERSION
OF
YOU

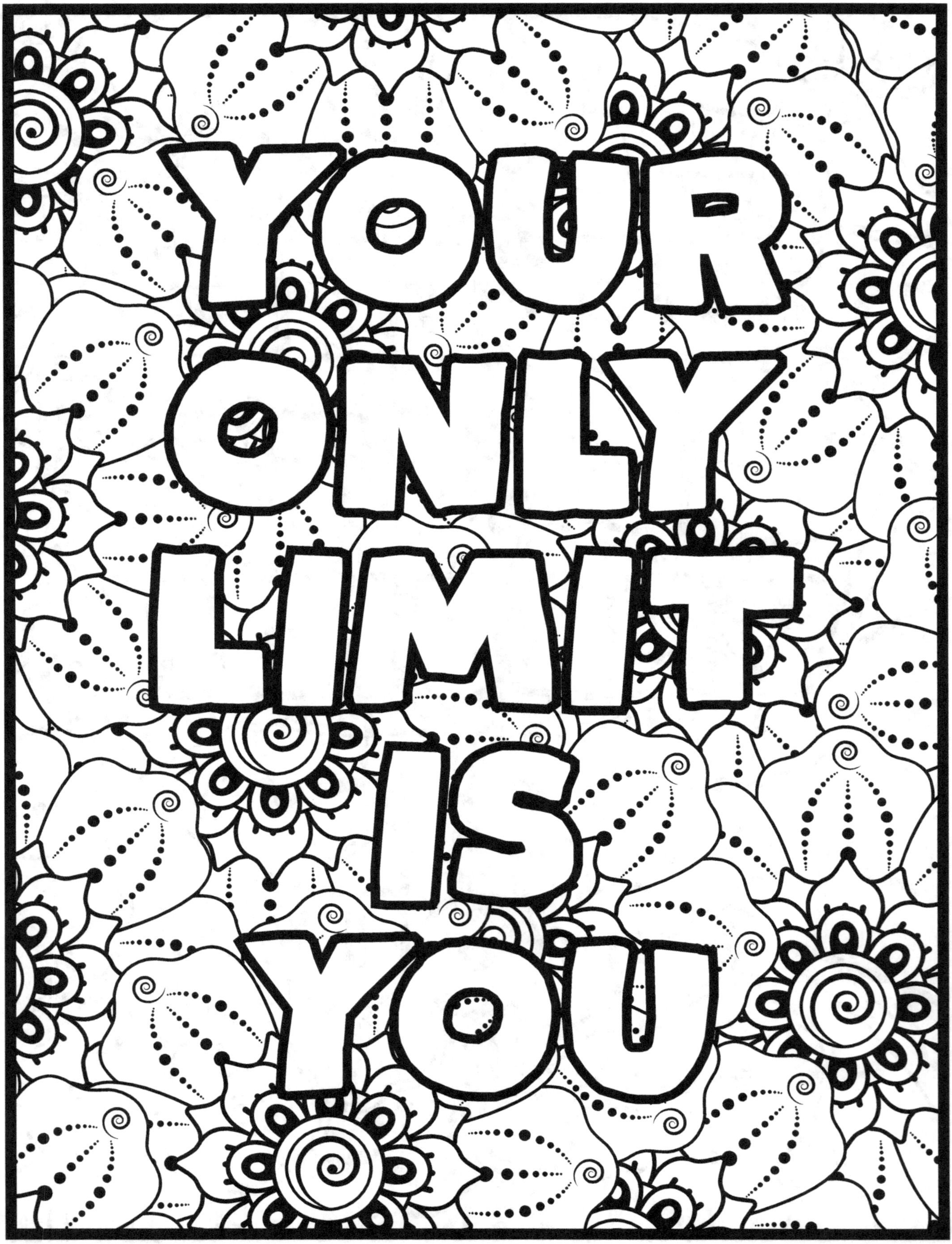
YOUR
ONLY
LIMIT
IS
YOU

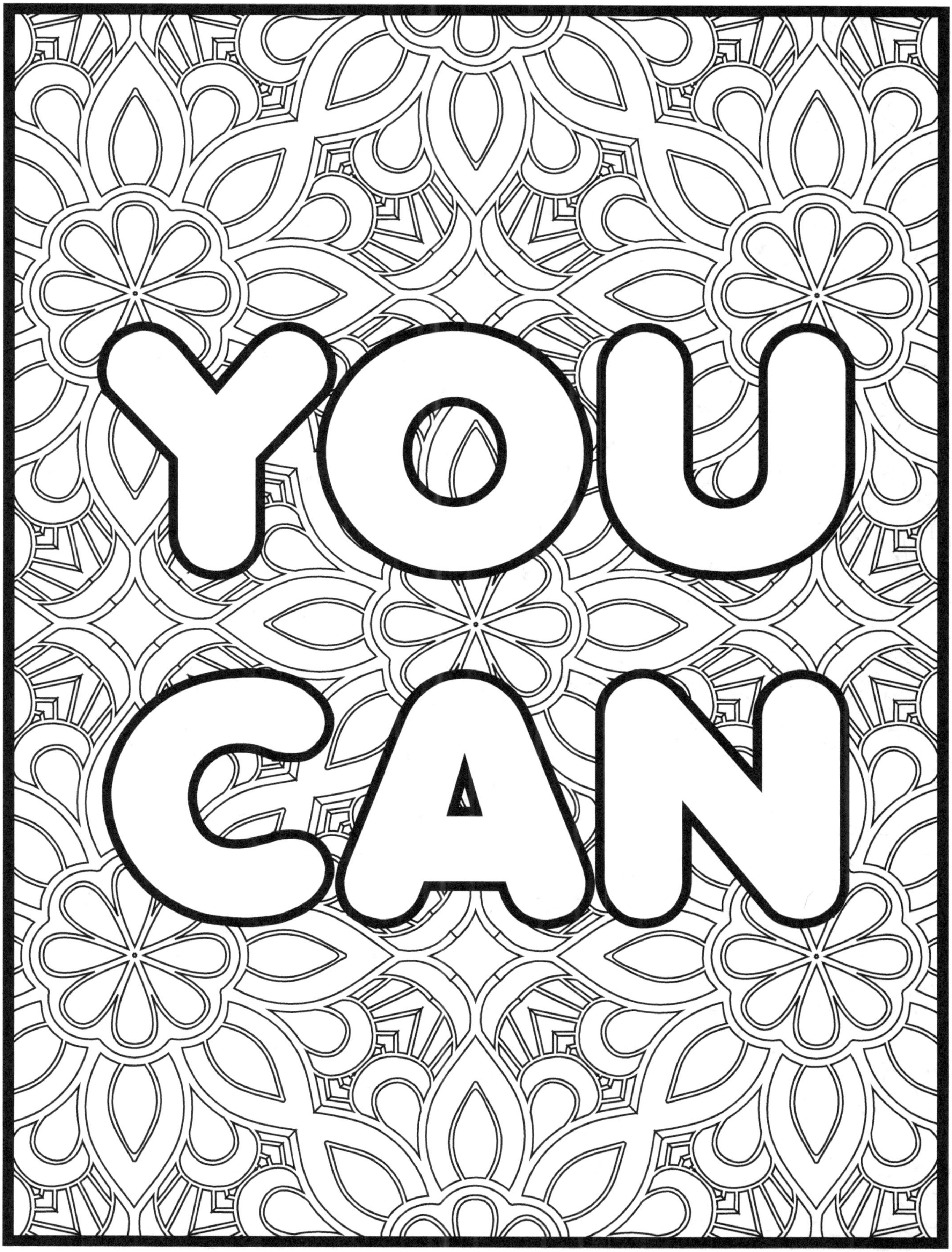
YOU
CAN

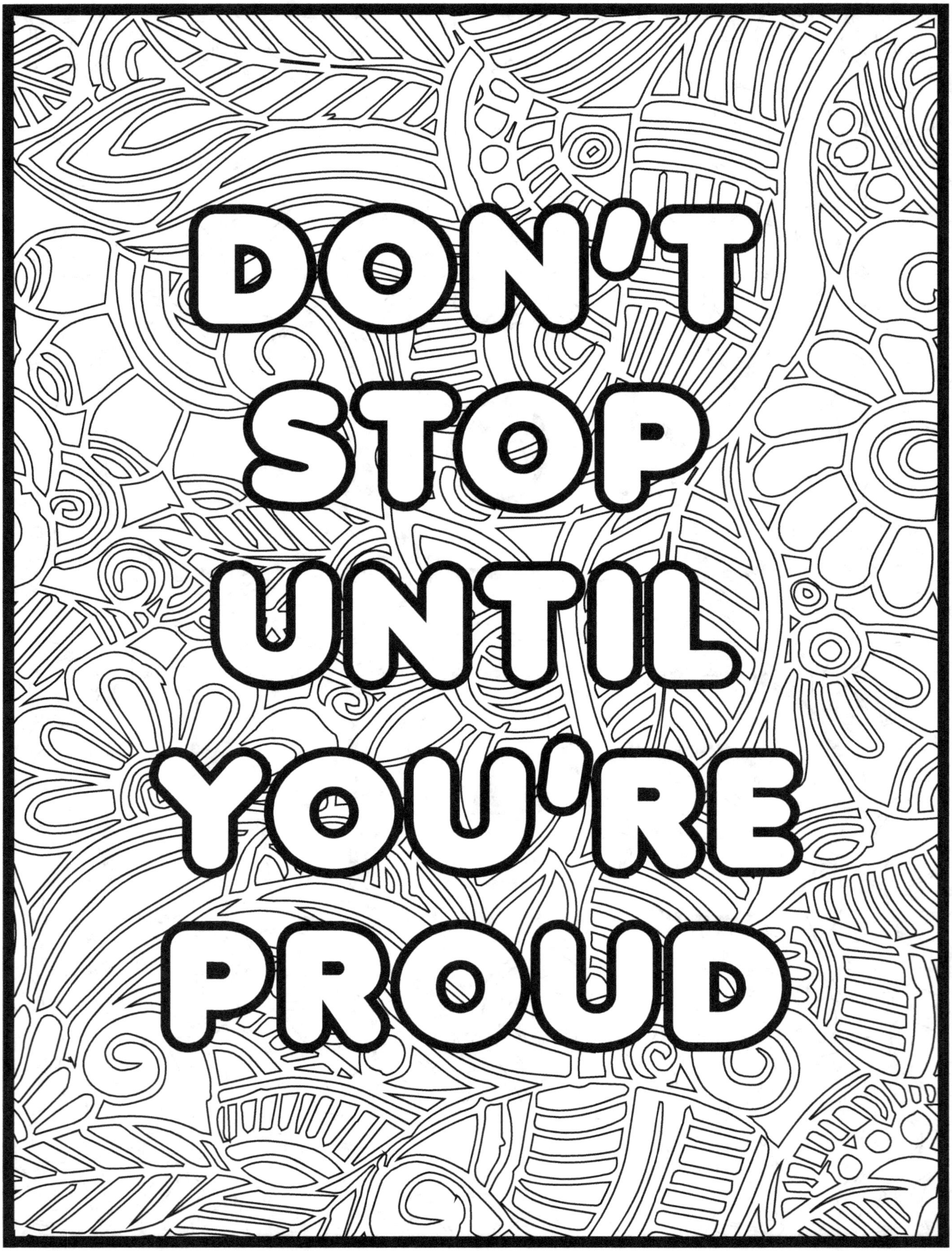
DON'T
STOP
UNTIL
YOU'RE
PROUD

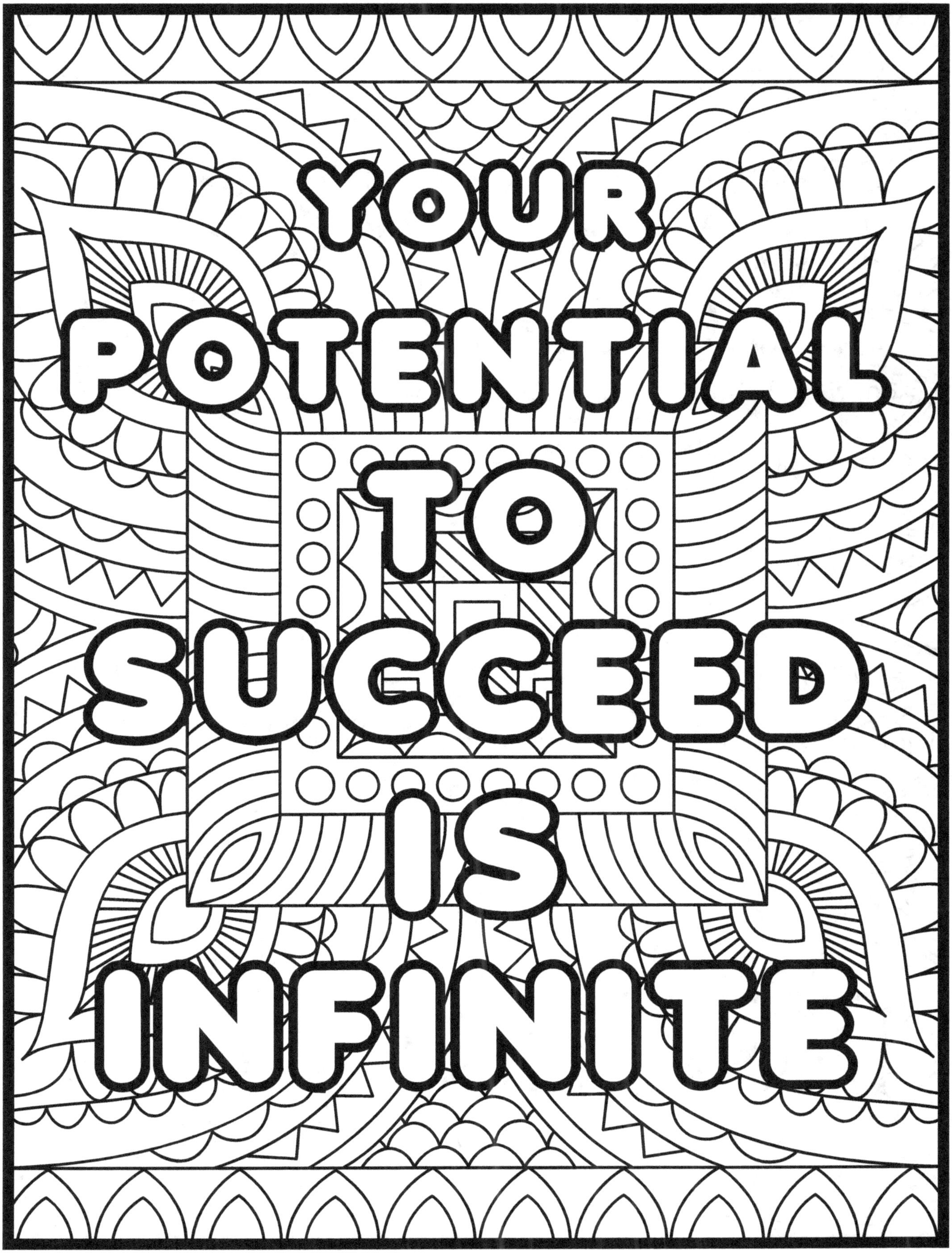
YOUR
POTENTIAL
TO
SUCCEED
IS
INFINITE

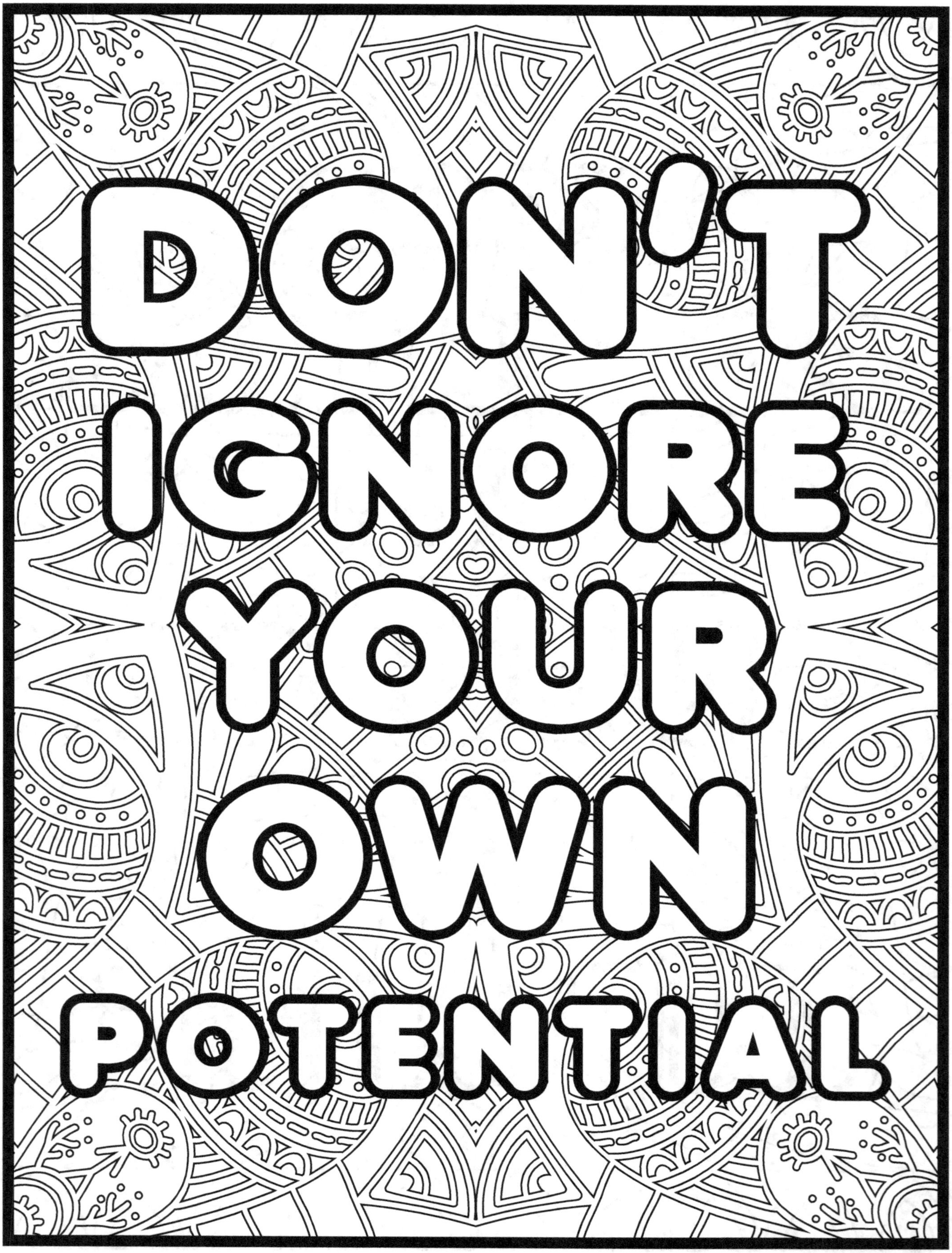
DON'T
IGNORE
YOUR
OWN
POTENTIAL

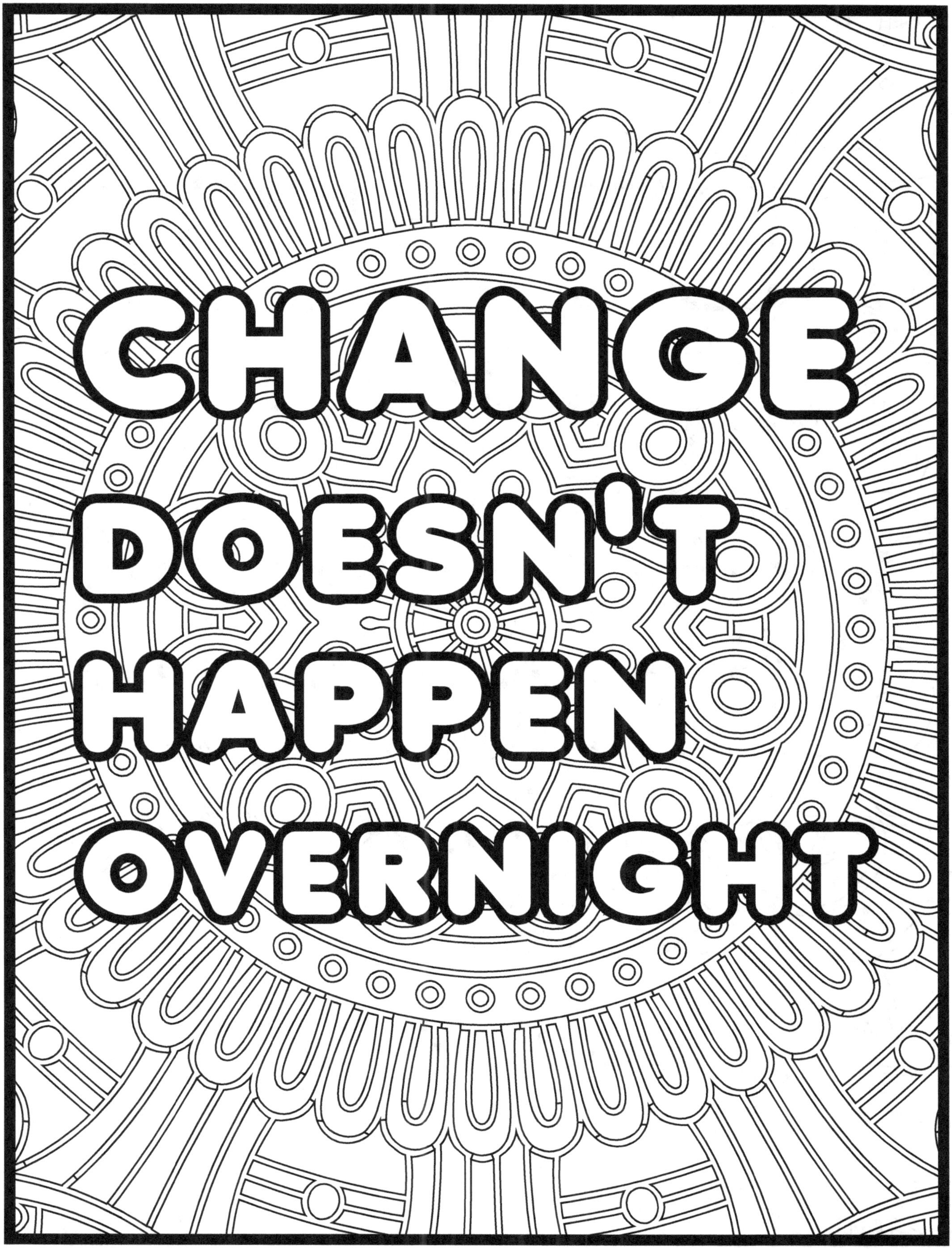
CHANGE
DOESN'T
HAPPEN
OVERNIGHT

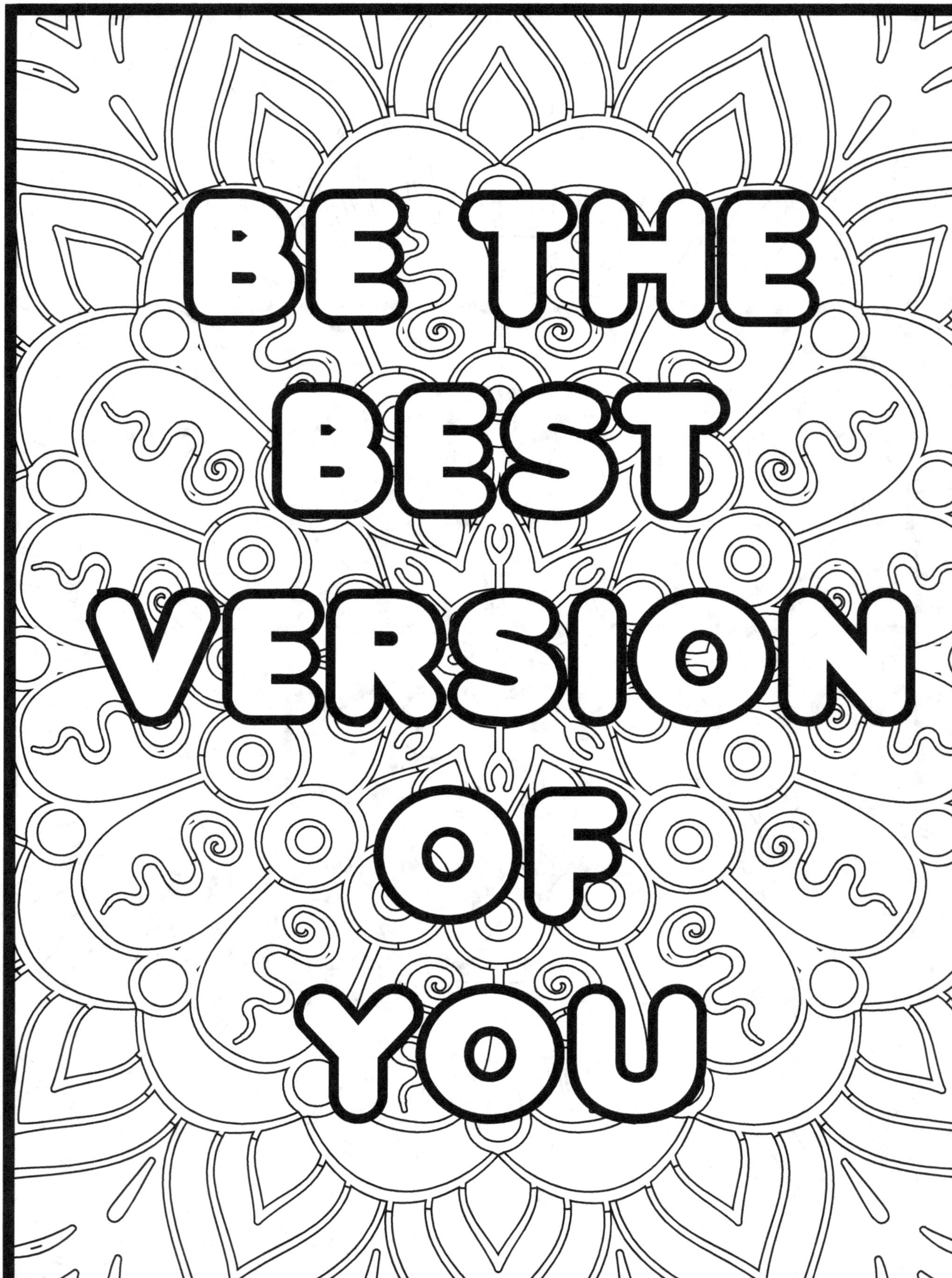
BE THE
BEST
VERSION
OF
YOU

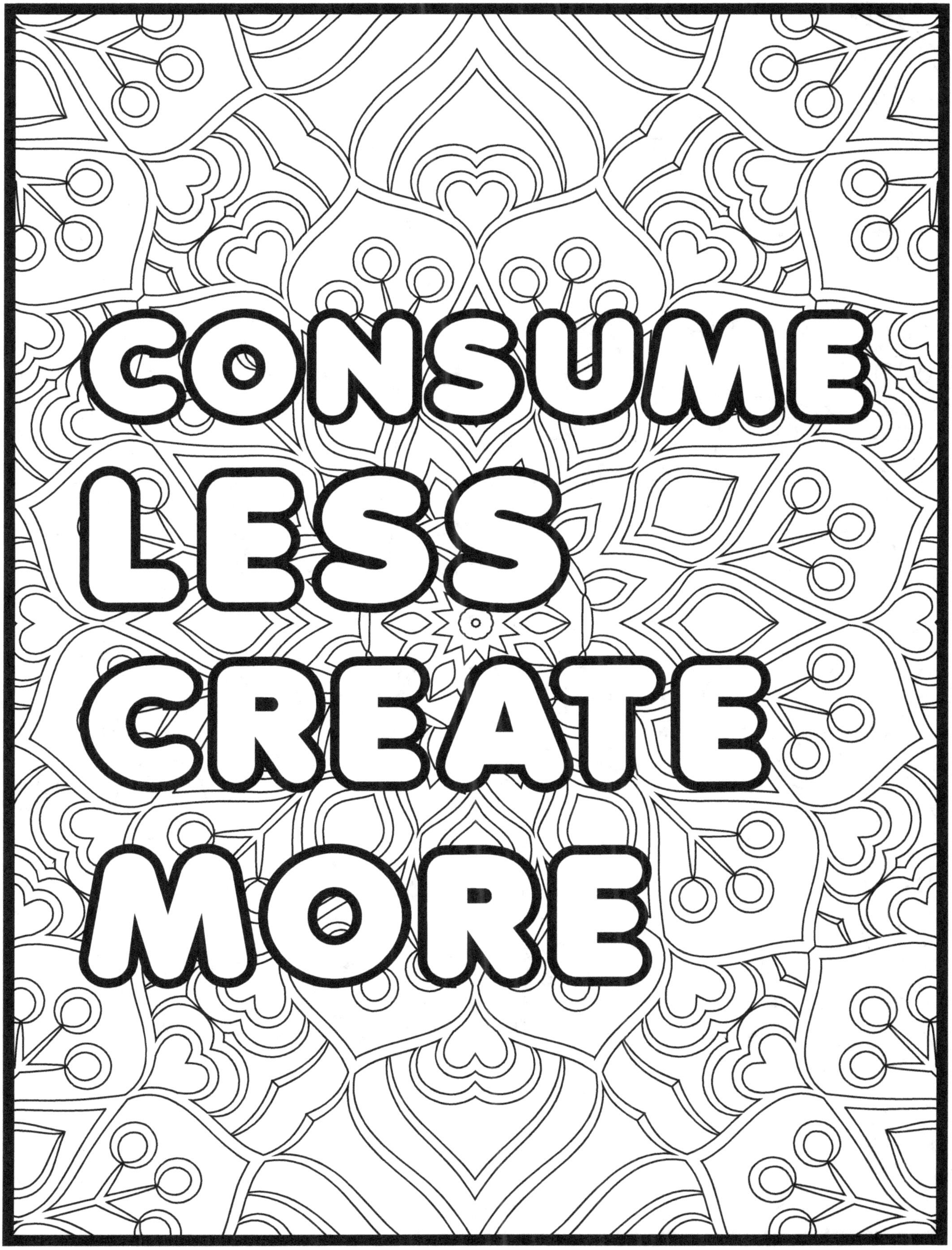
CONSUME
LESS
CREATE
MORE

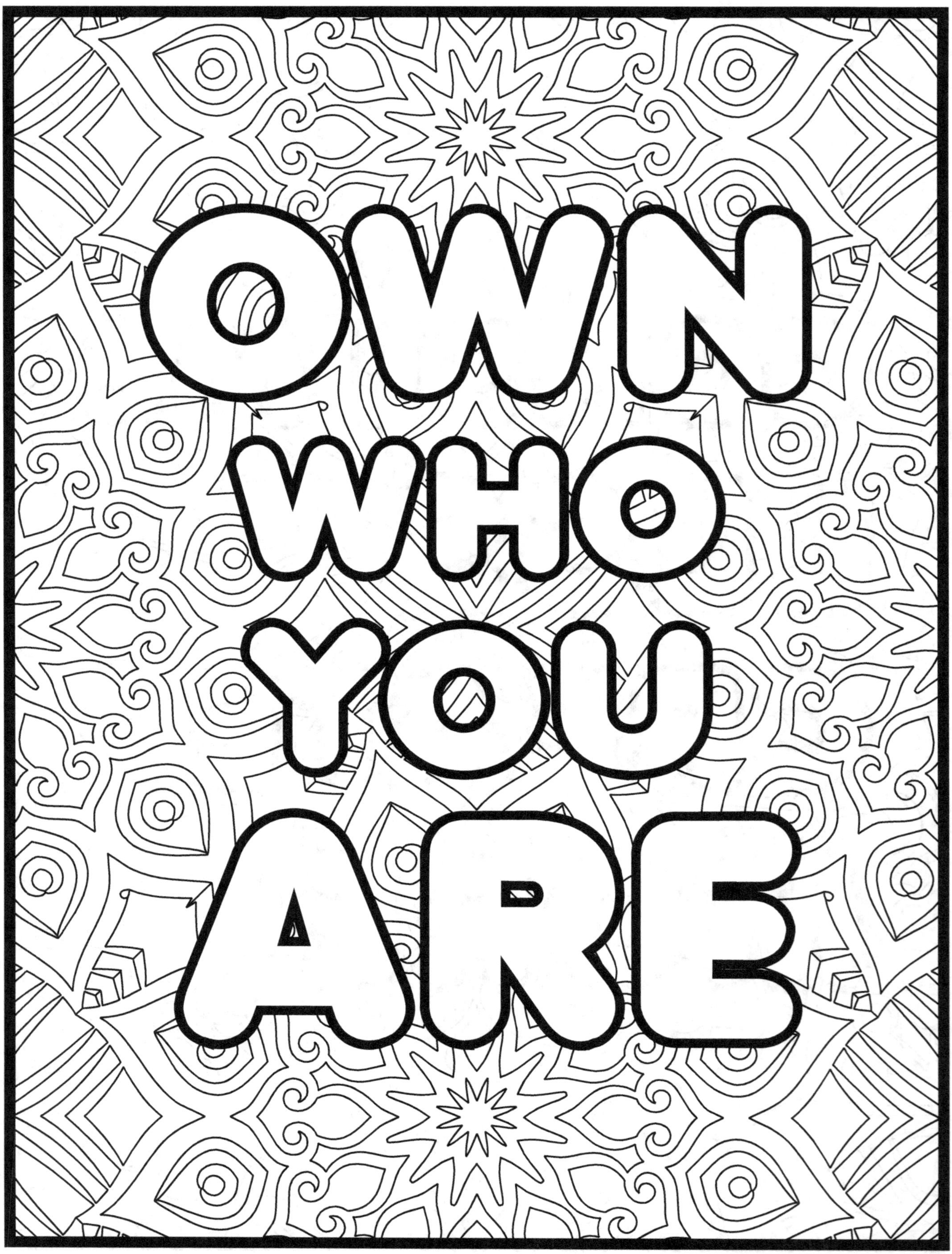
OWN
WHO
YOU
ARE

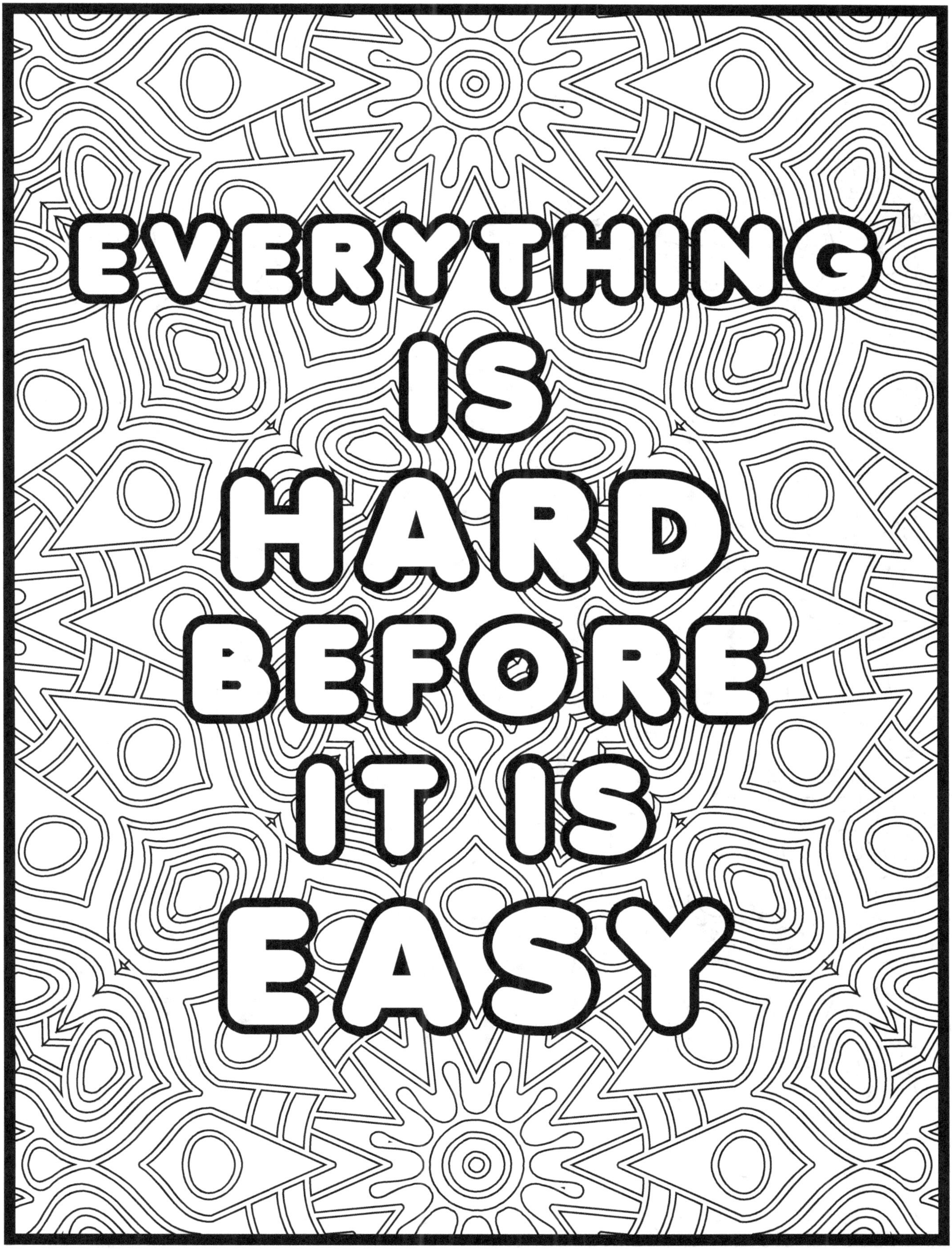
EVERYTHING
IS
HARD
BEFORE
IT IS
EASY

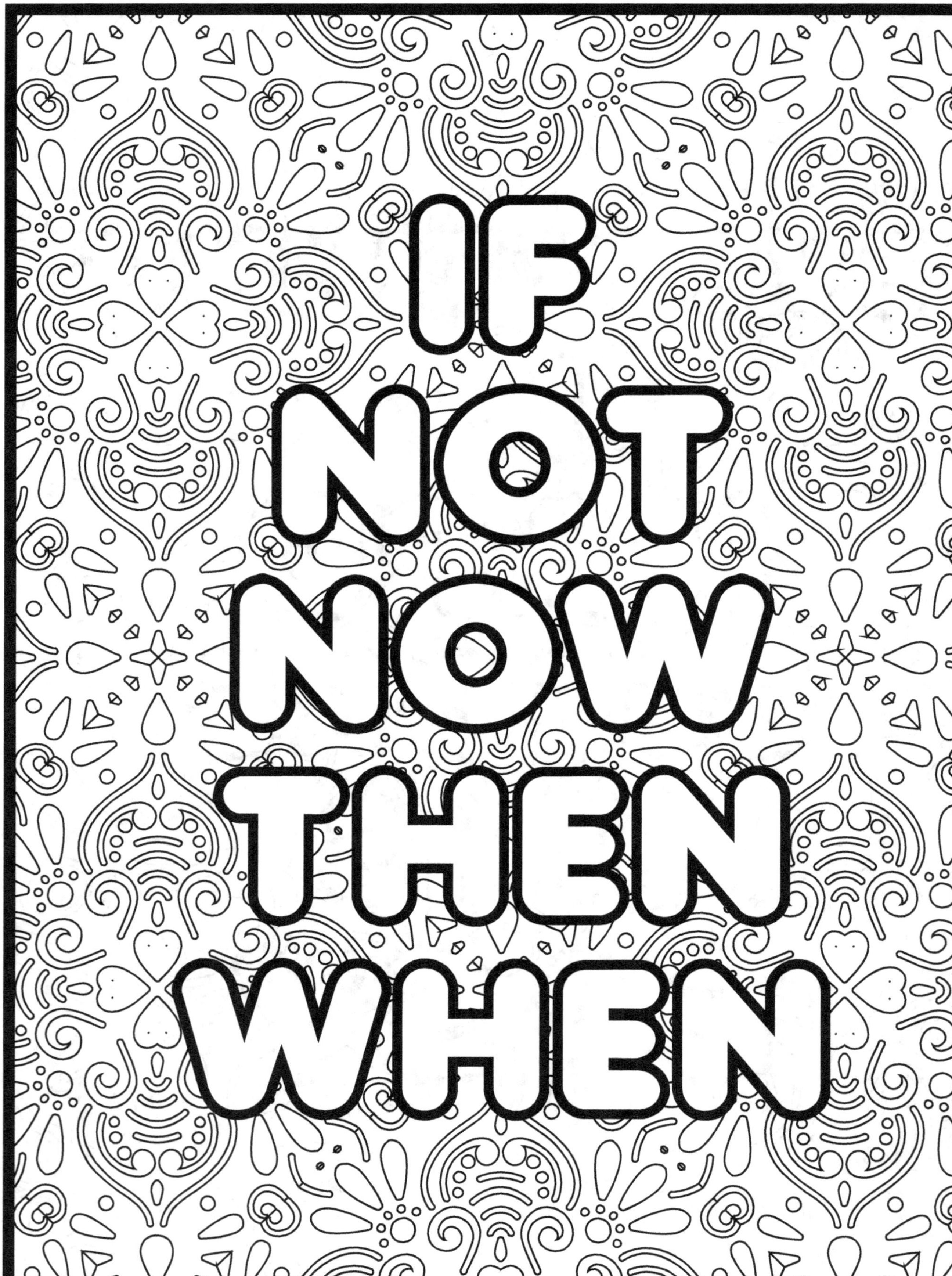
IF
NOT
NOW
THEN
WHEN

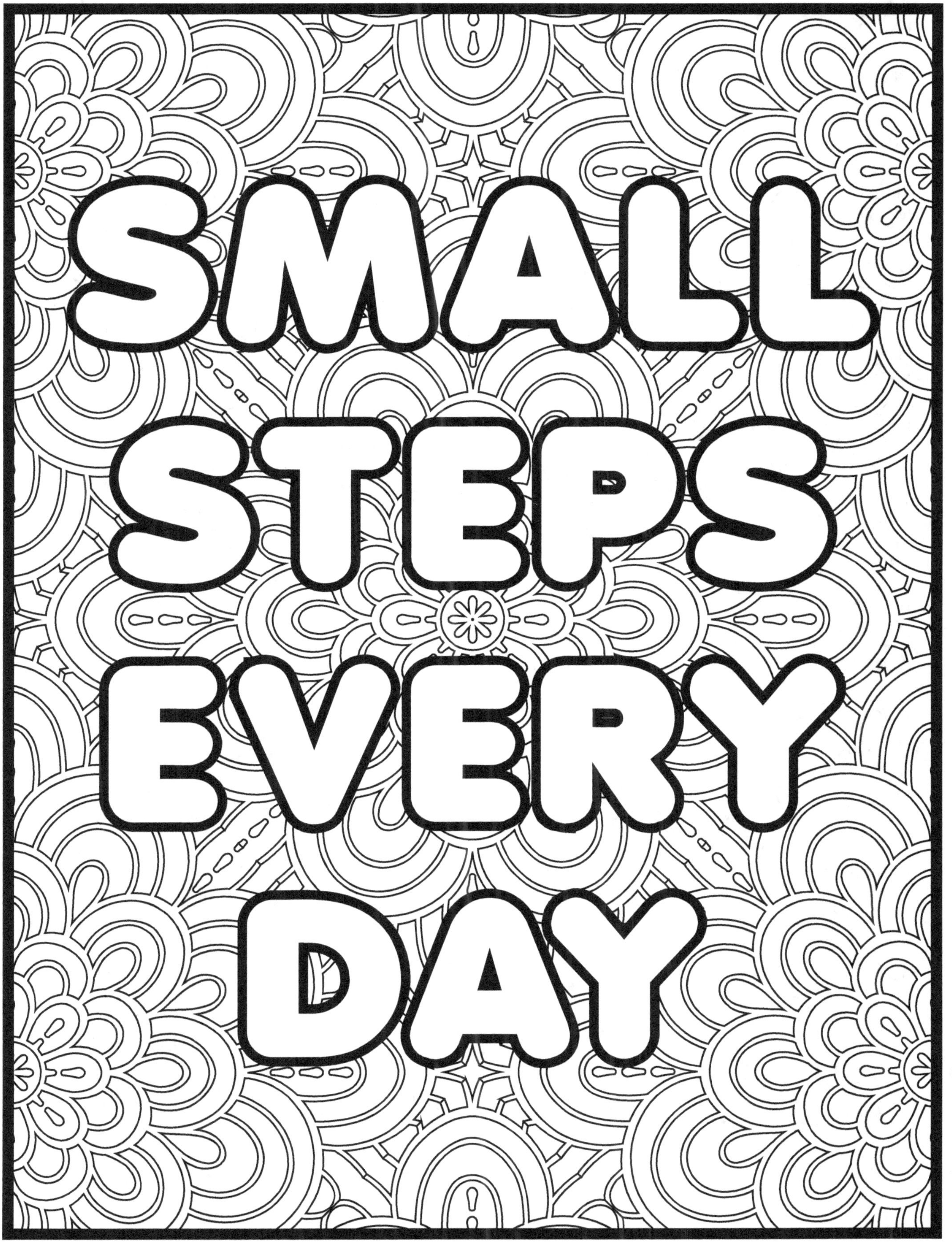
SMALL
STEPS
EVERY
DAY

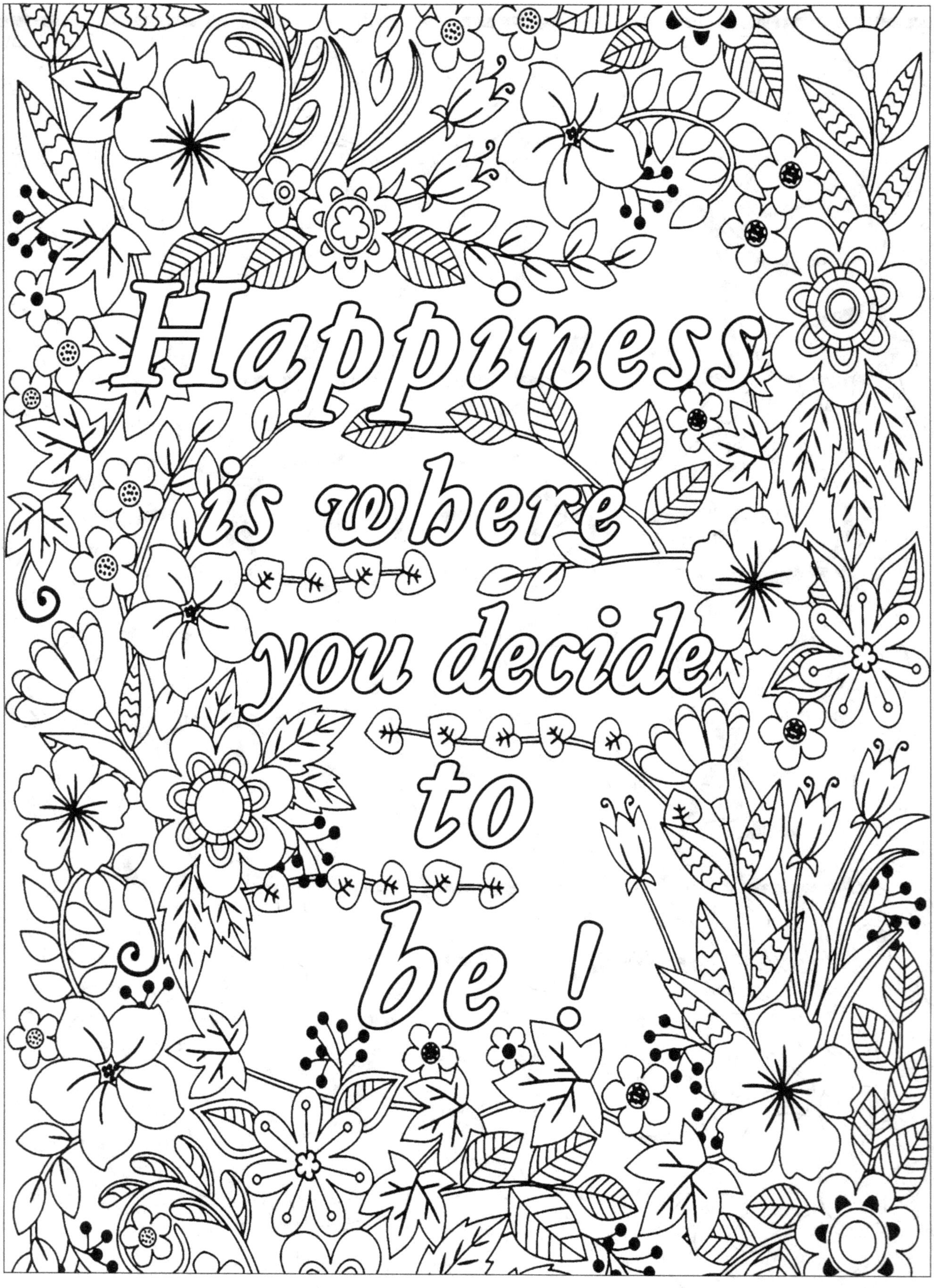
Happiness
is where
you decide
to
be !

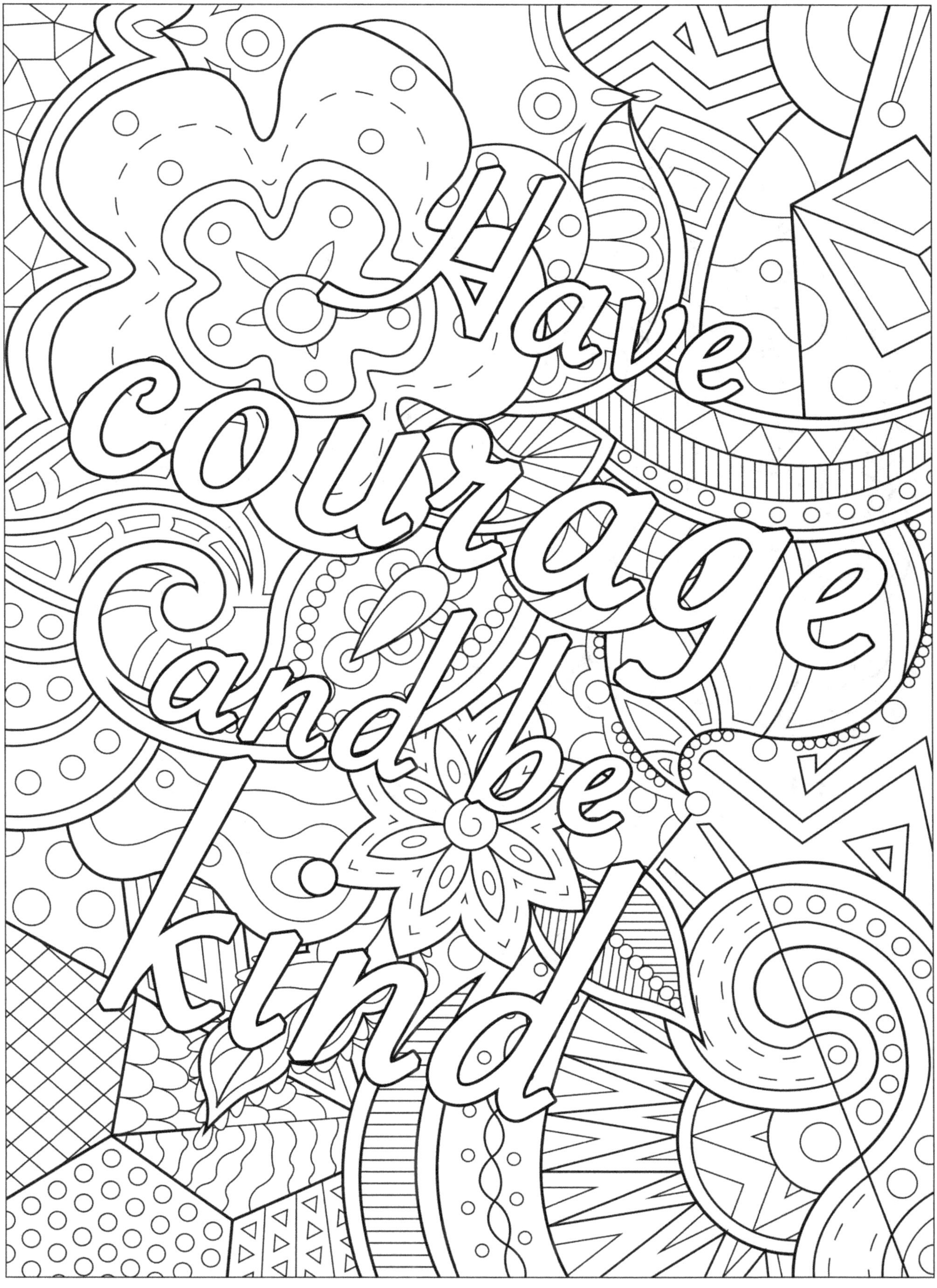
Have courage and be kind

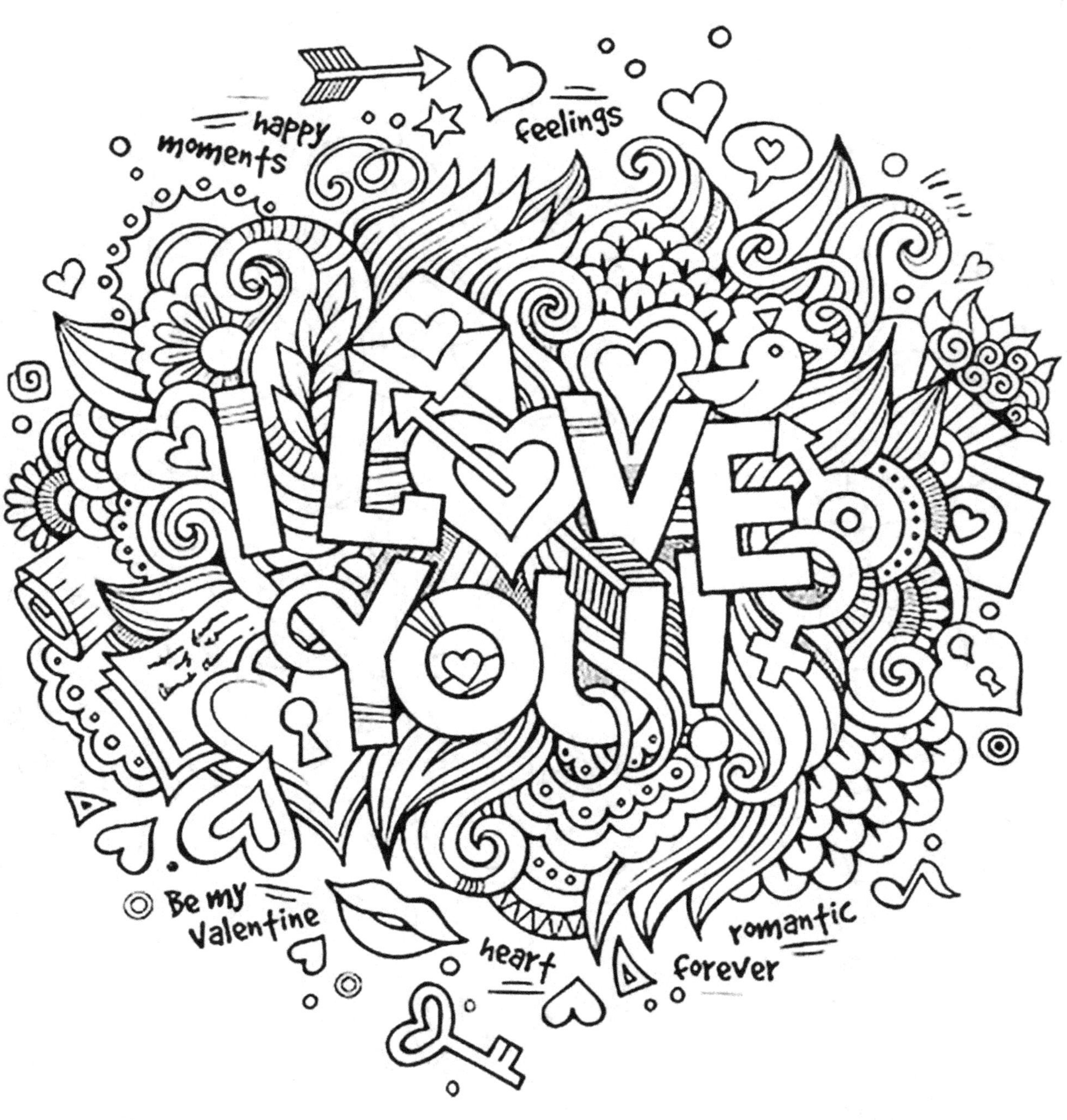
happy
moments
feelings
I LOVE YOU!
Be my
Valentine
heart
romantic
forever

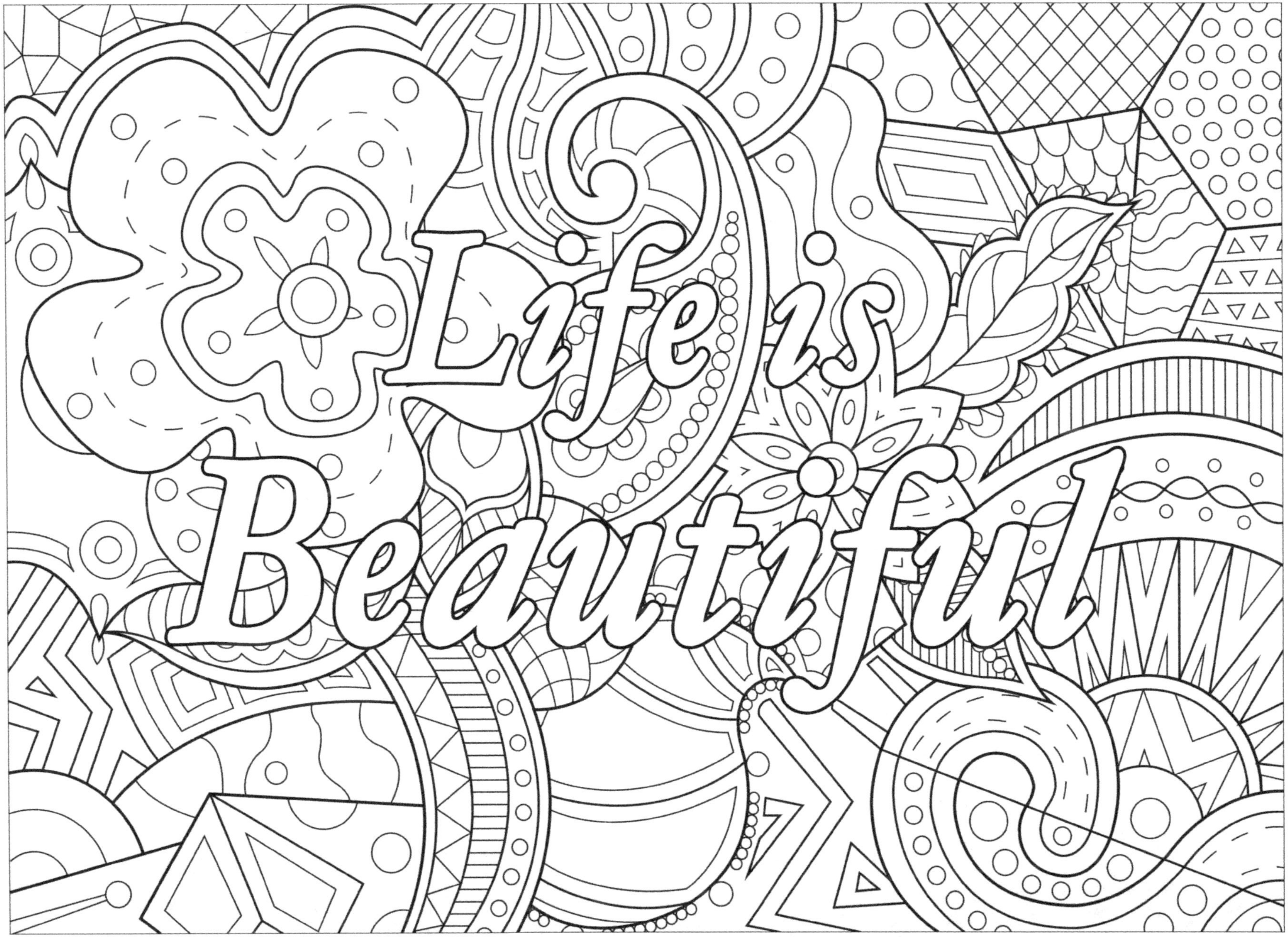
Life is
Beautiful

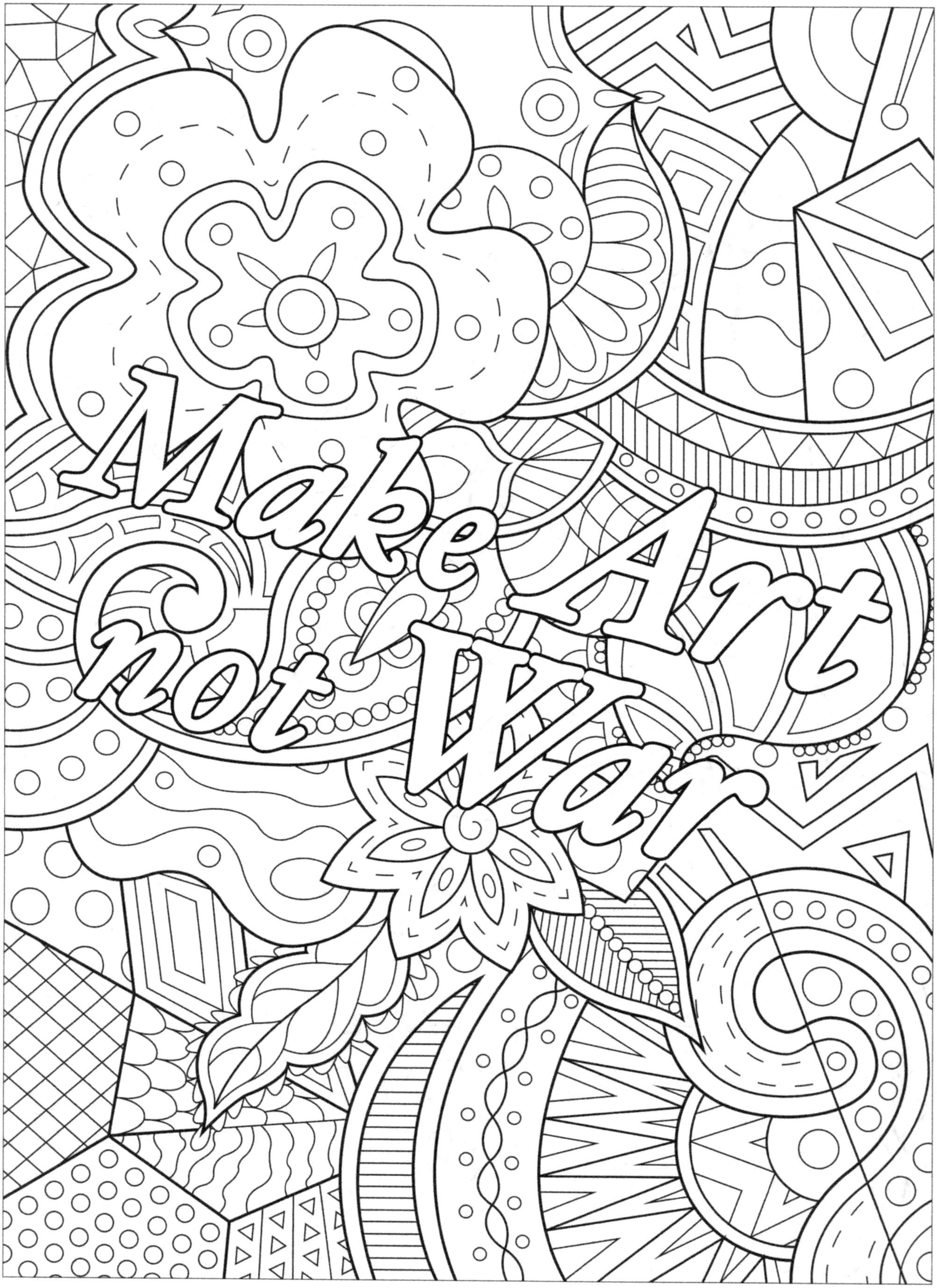
Make Art
not War

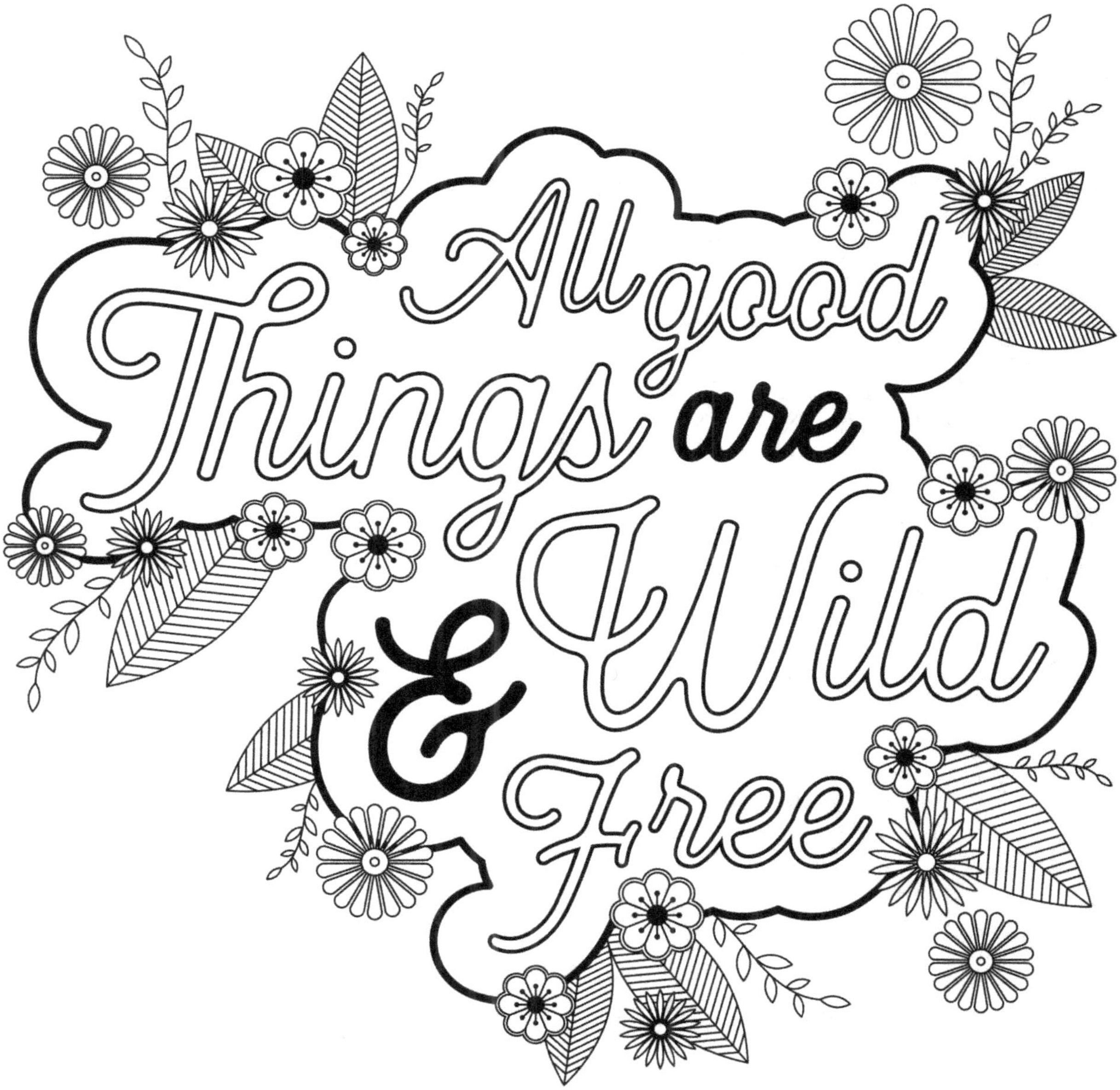
All good
Things are
& Wild
Free

Good Morning

never forget how awesome you are

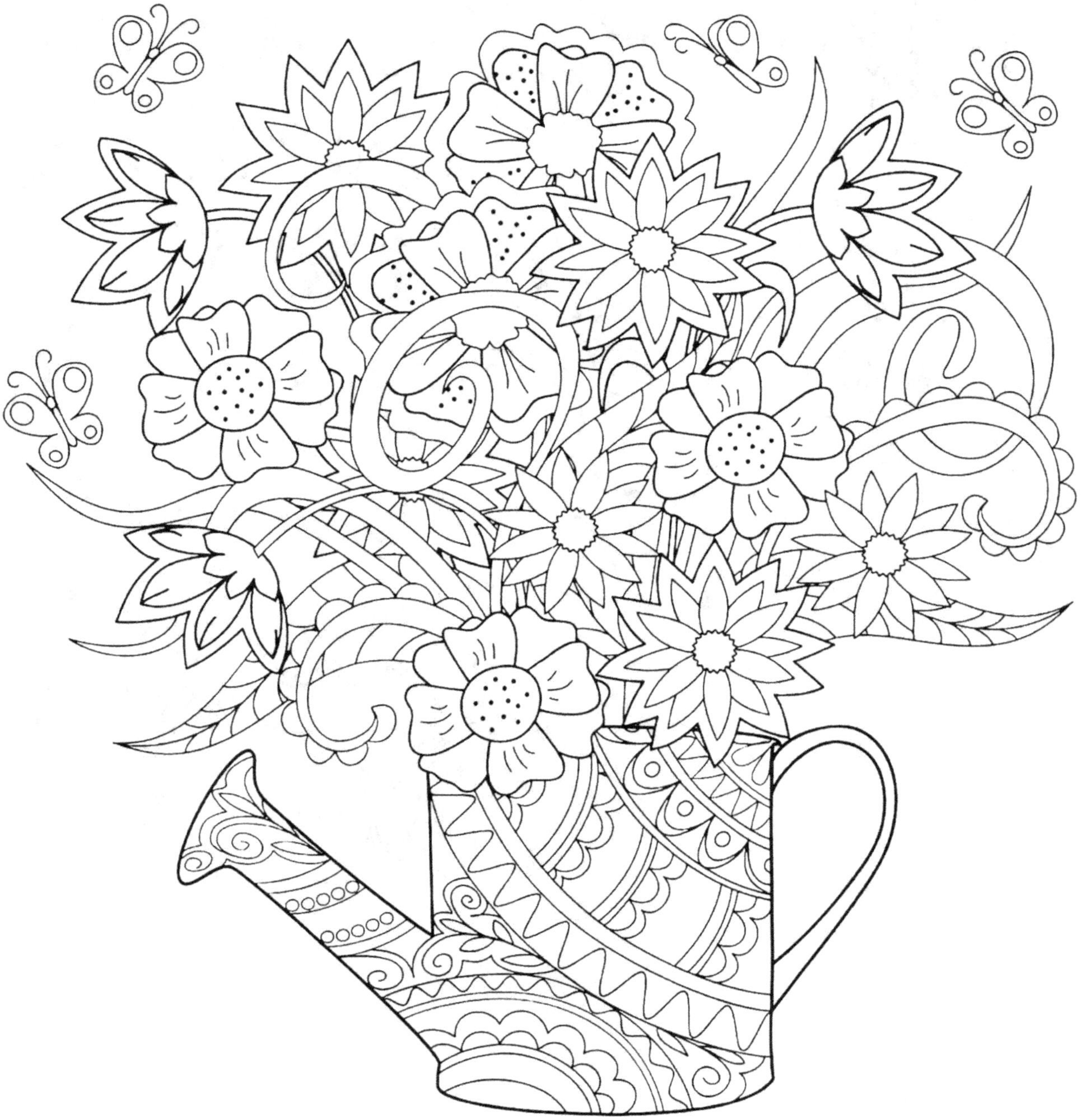

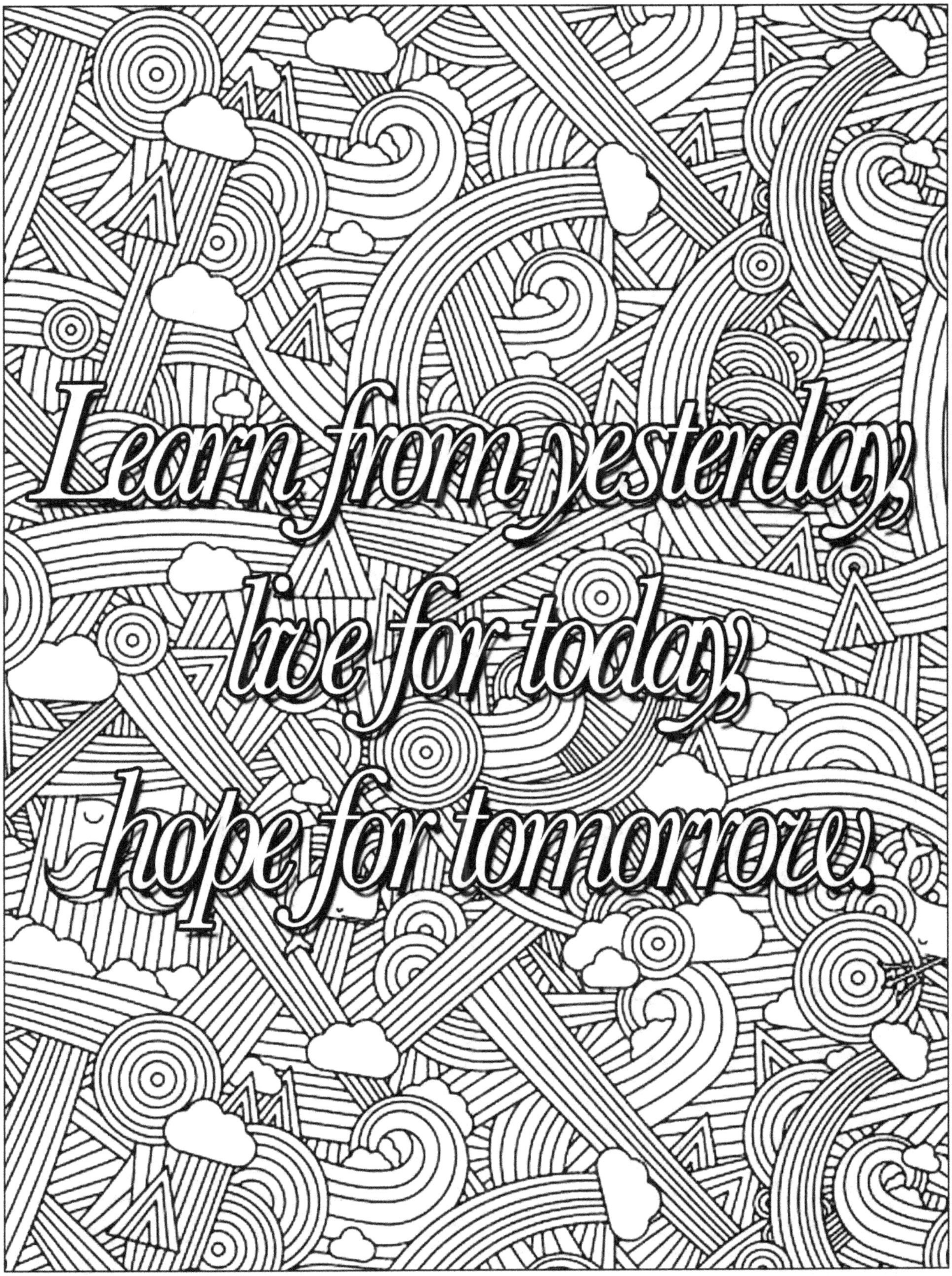
Learn from yesterday,
live for today,
hope for tomorrow.

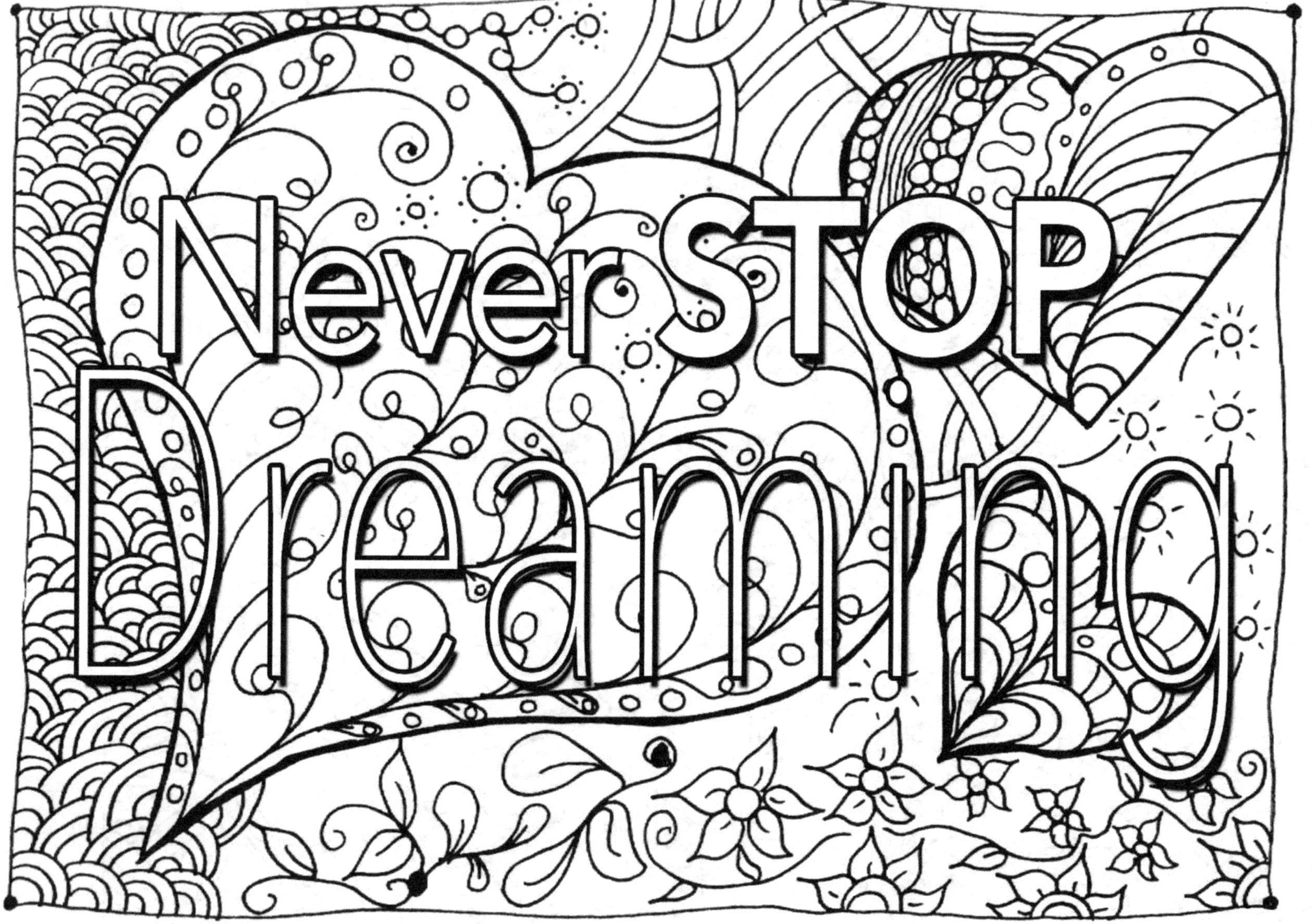
Never STOP
Dreaming

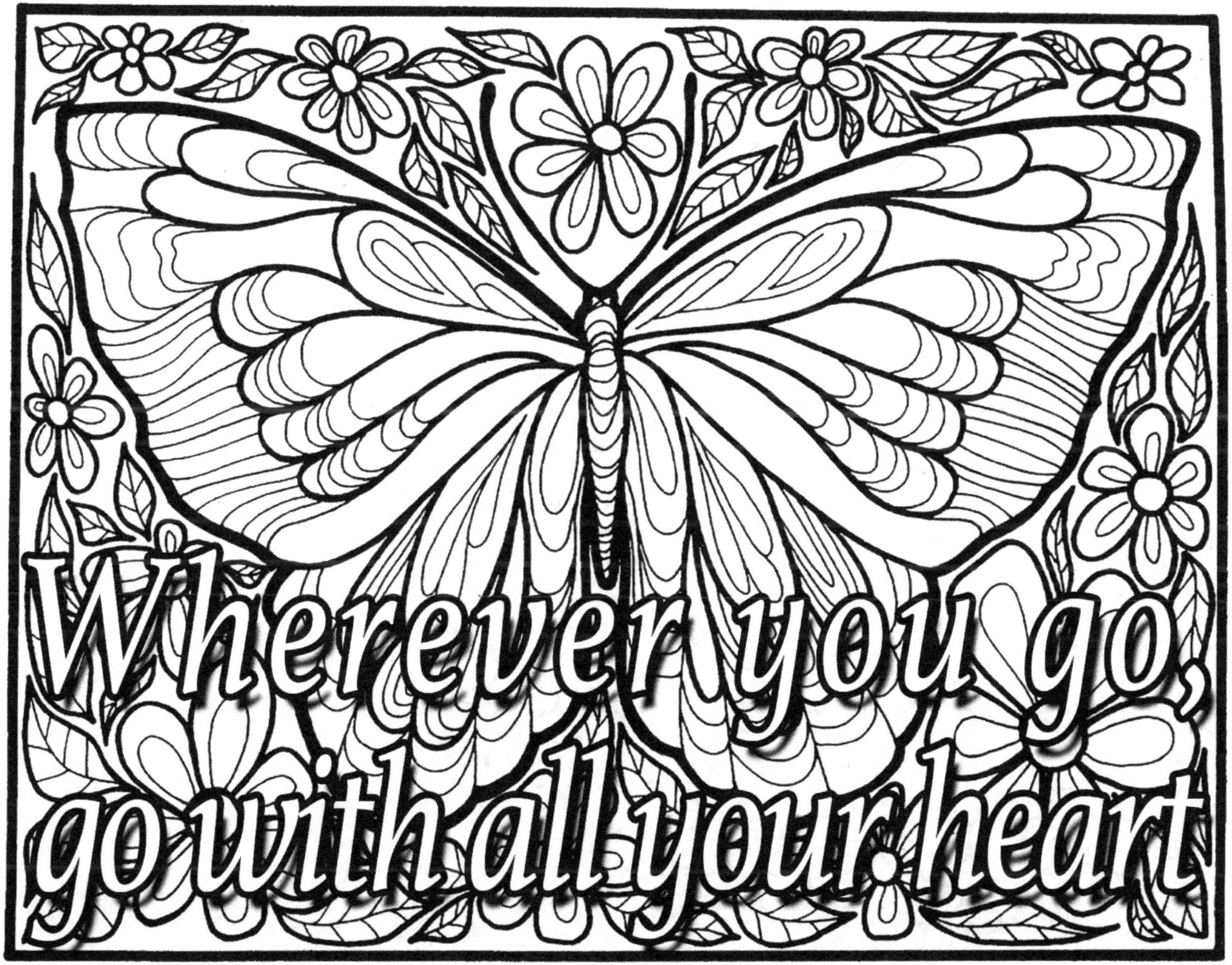
Wherever you go,
go with all your heart

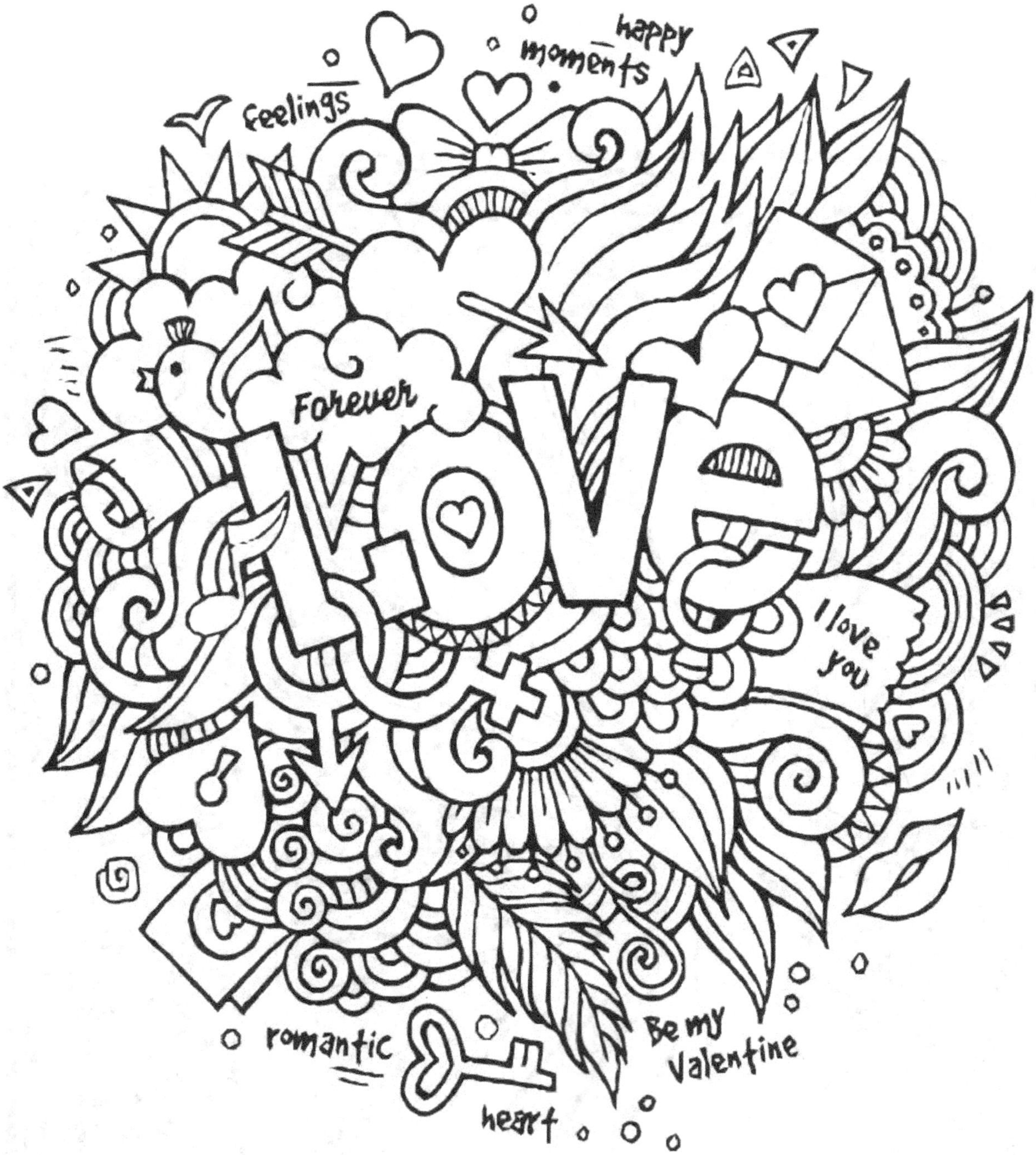
happy
moments
feelings
Forever
Love
I love
you
romantic
Be my
Valentine
heart

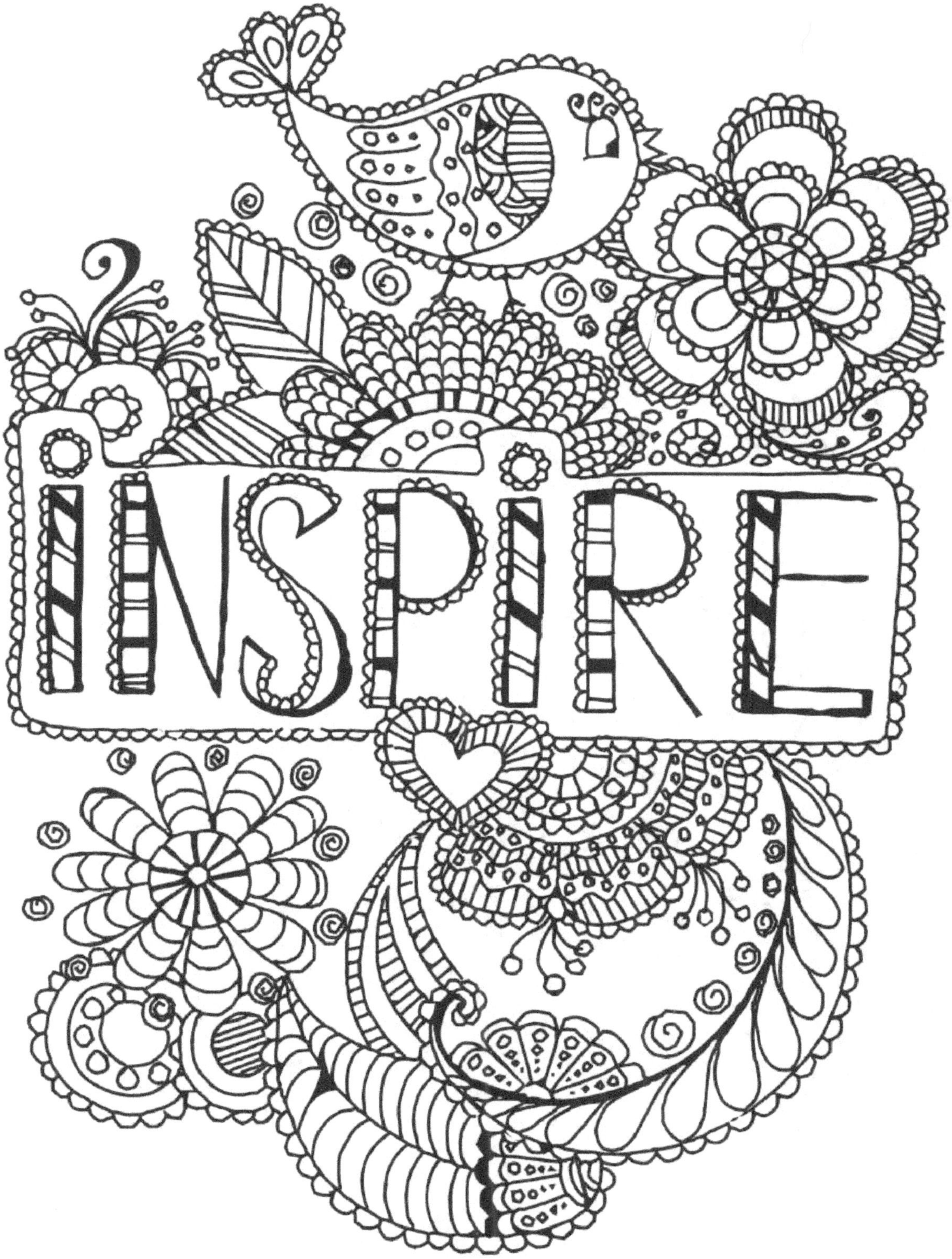
INSPIRE

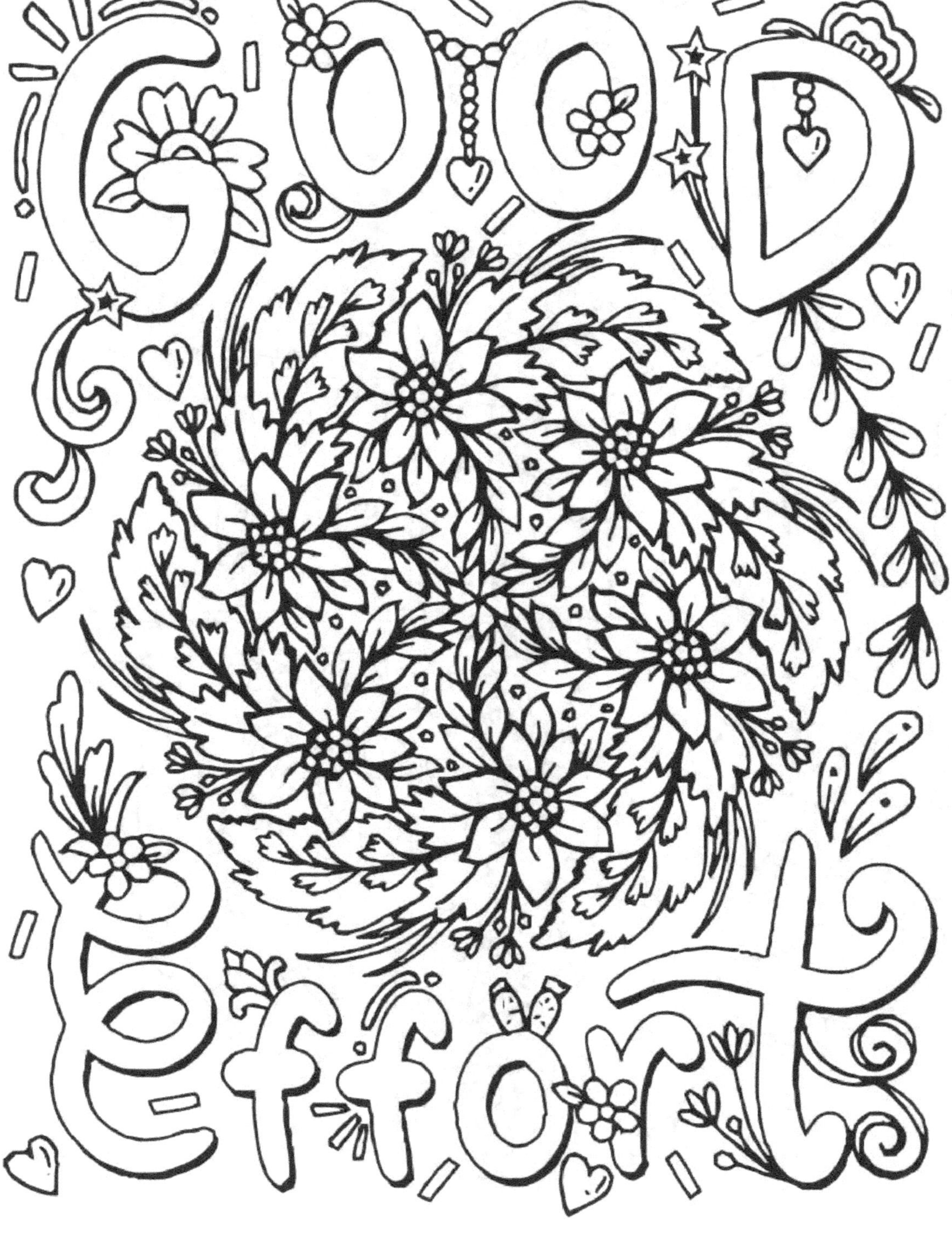
Good
Effort

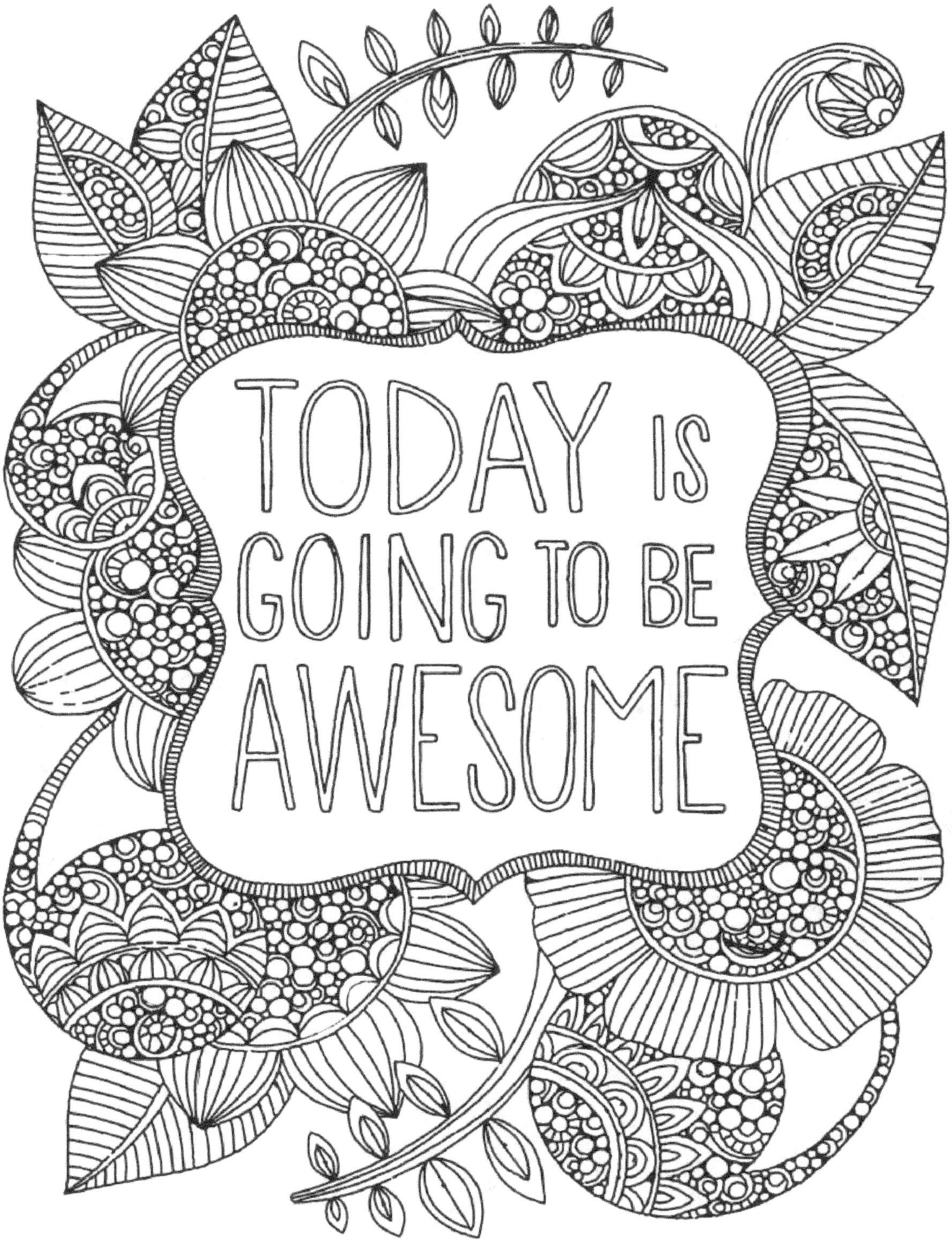
TODAY IS
GOING TO BE
AWESOME

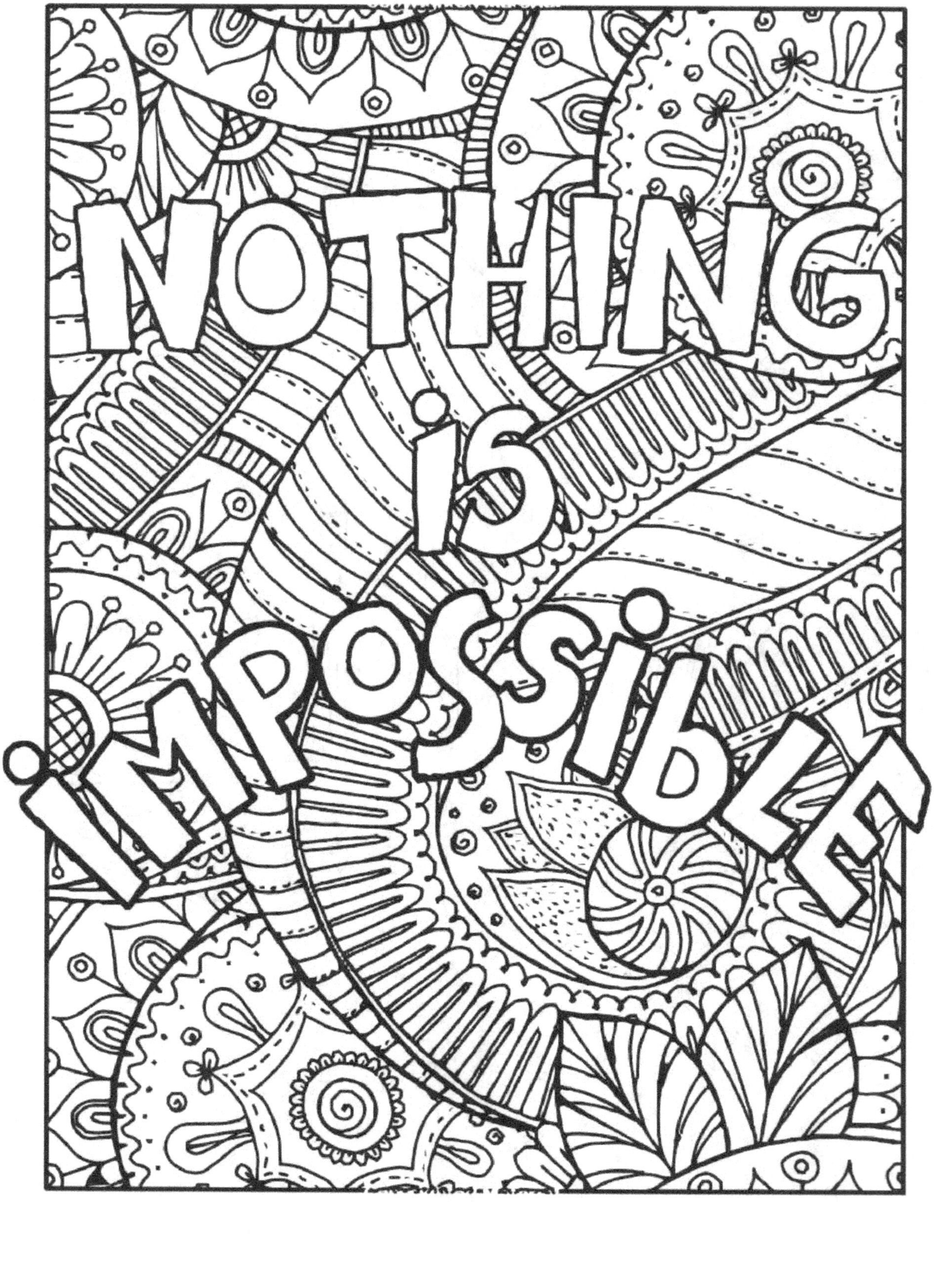
NOTHING
IS
IMPOSSIBLE

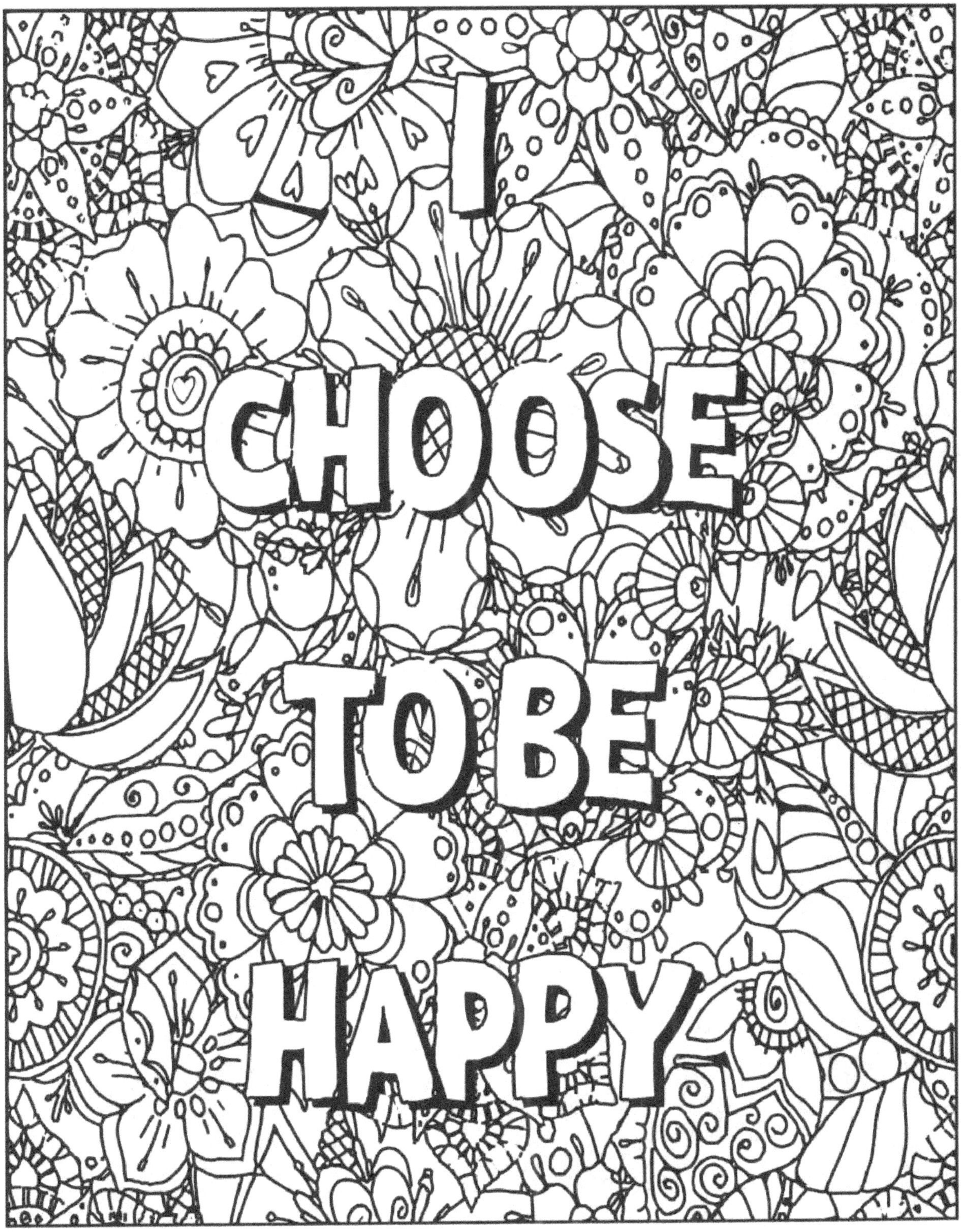
I
CHOOSE
TO BE
HAPPY

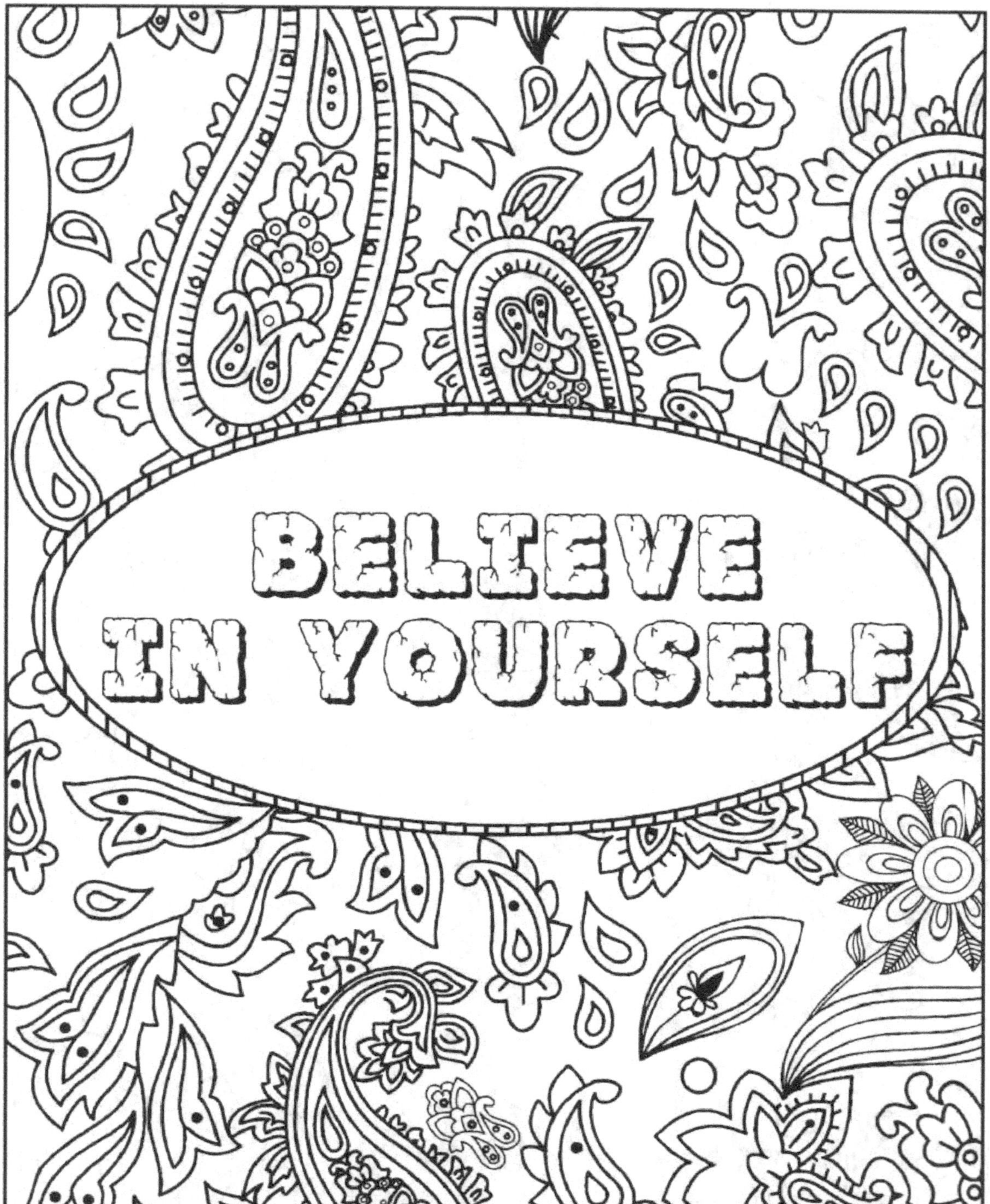
BELIEVE IN YOURSELF

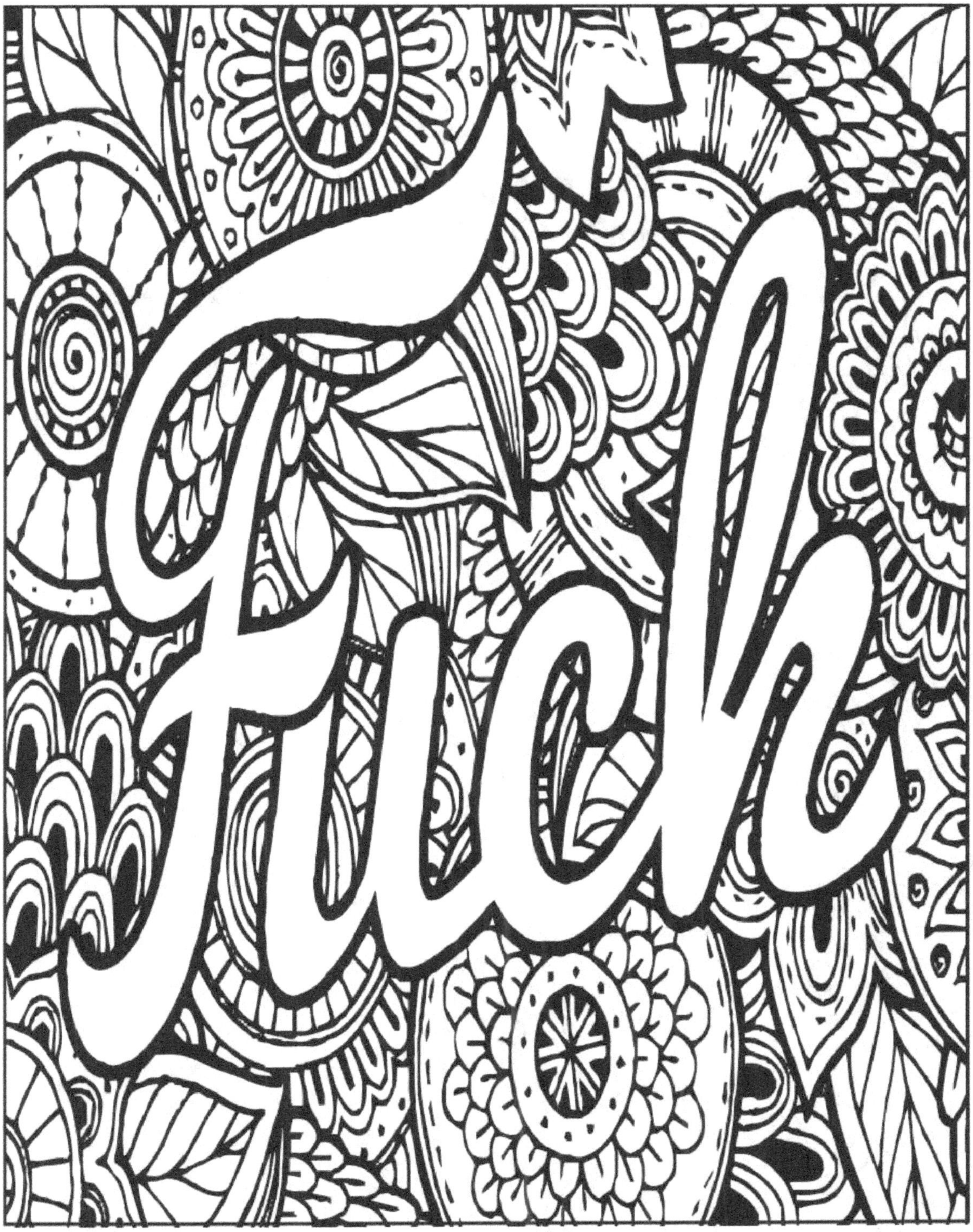
Fuck

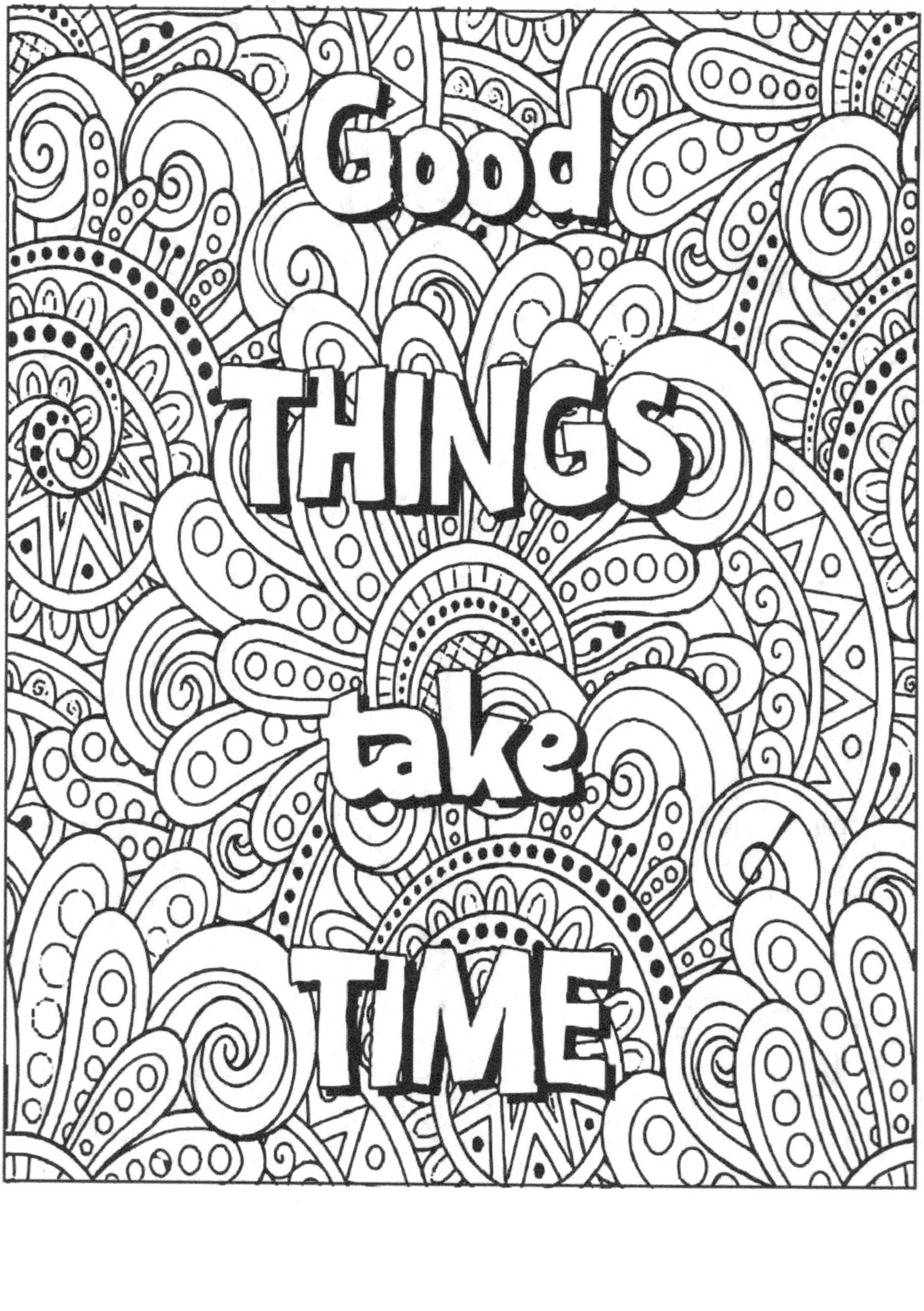
Good
THINGS
take
TIME

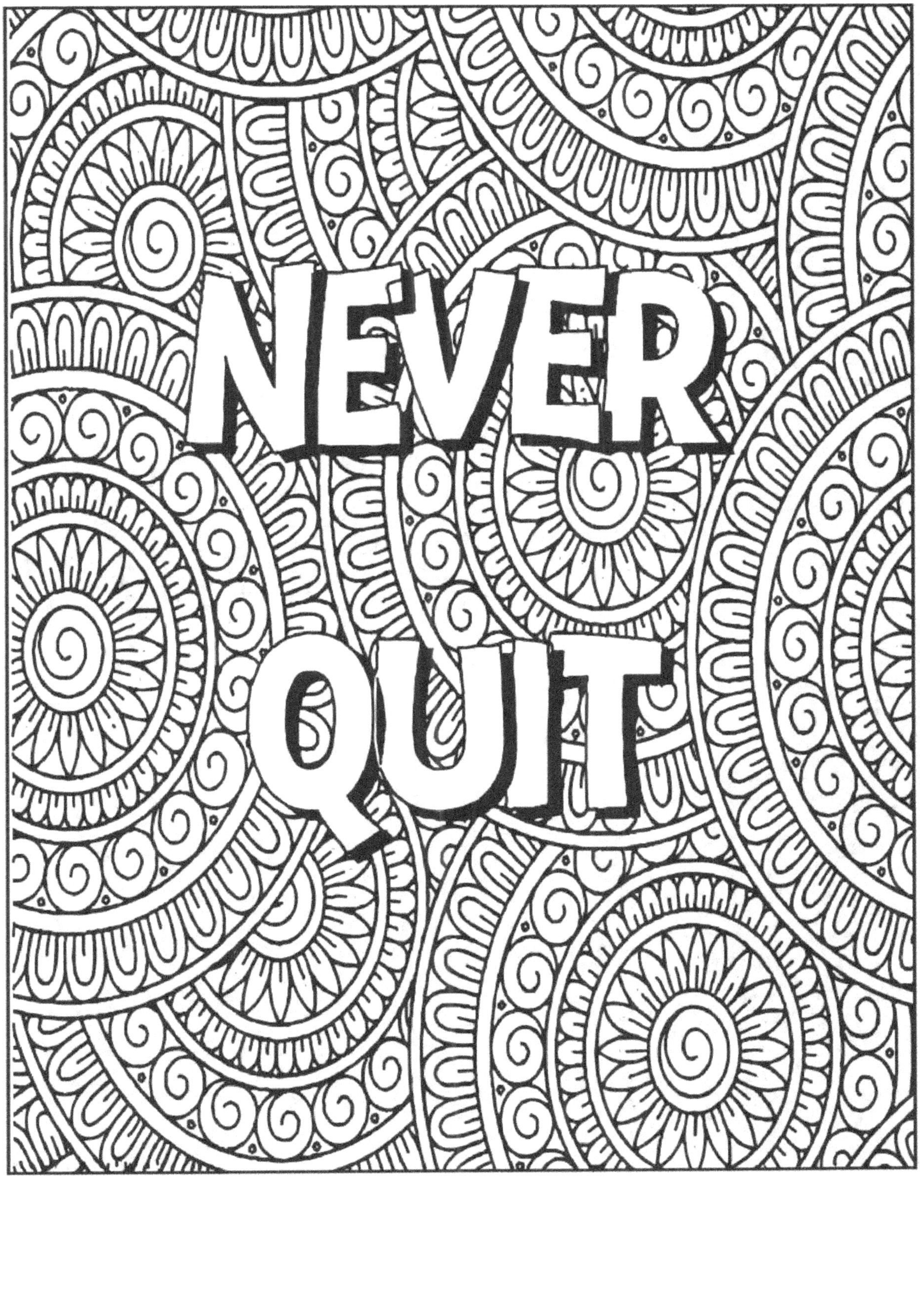
NEVER
QUIT

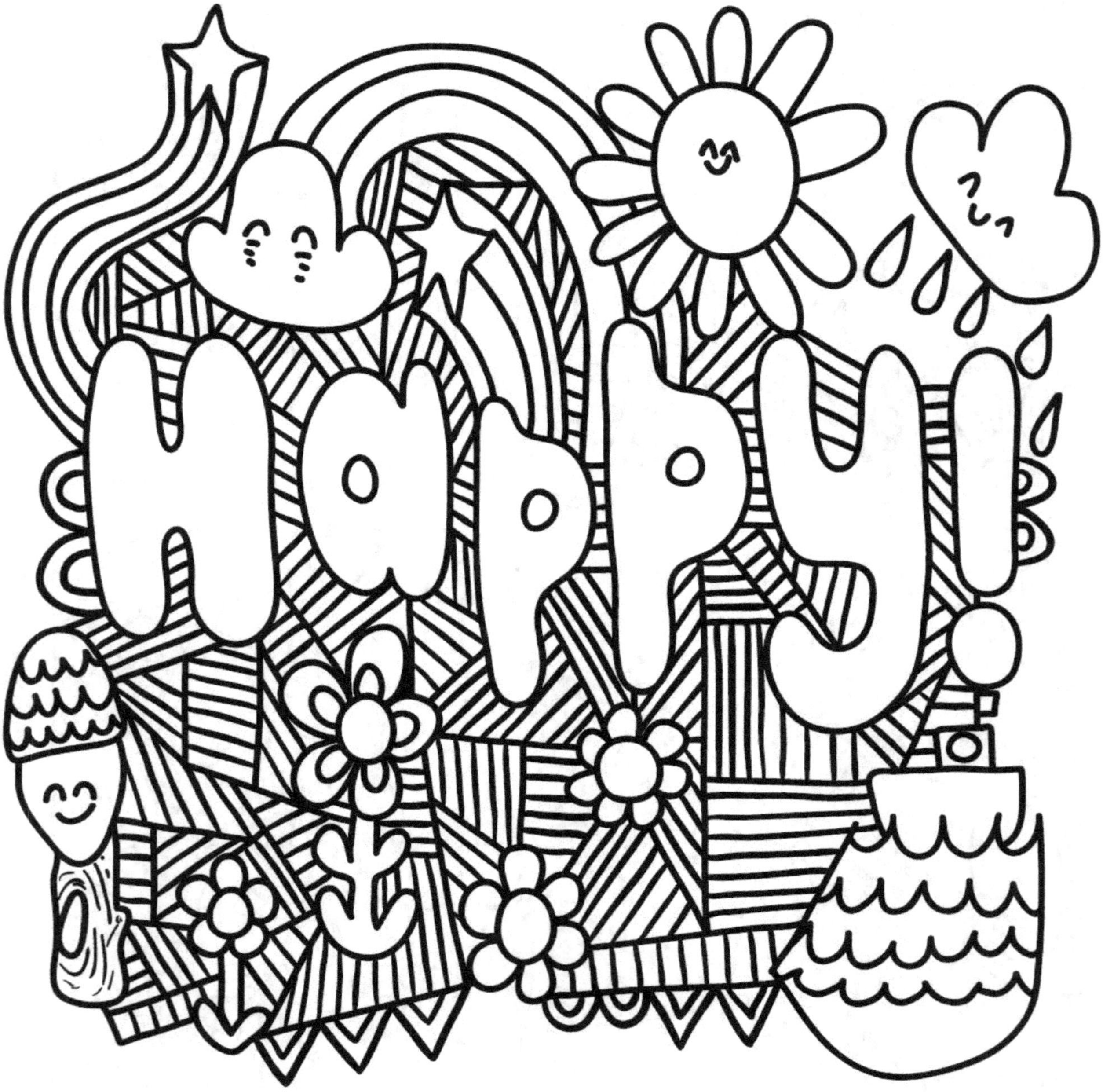
HAPPY!

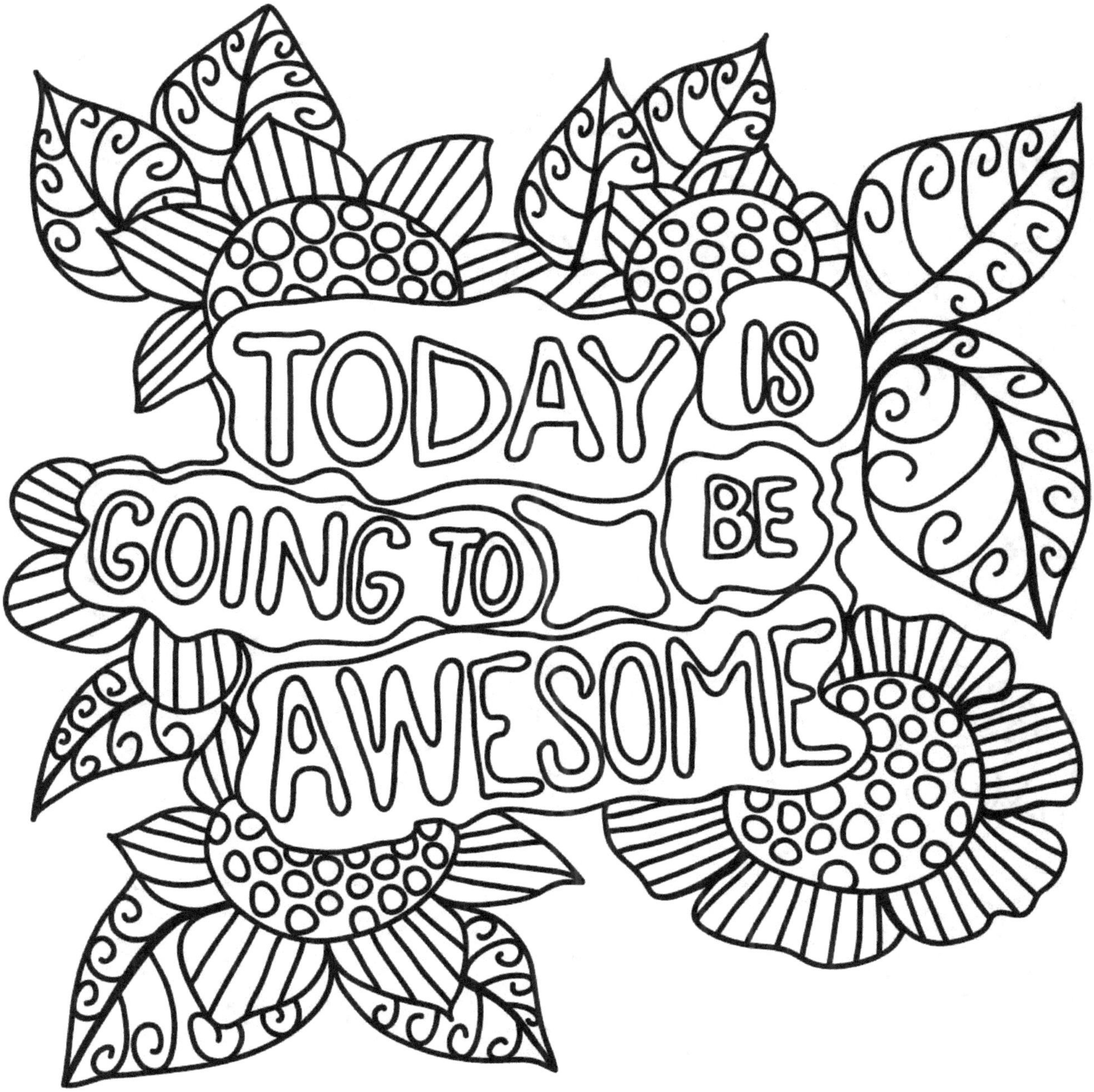
TODAY IS
GOING TO BE
AWESOME

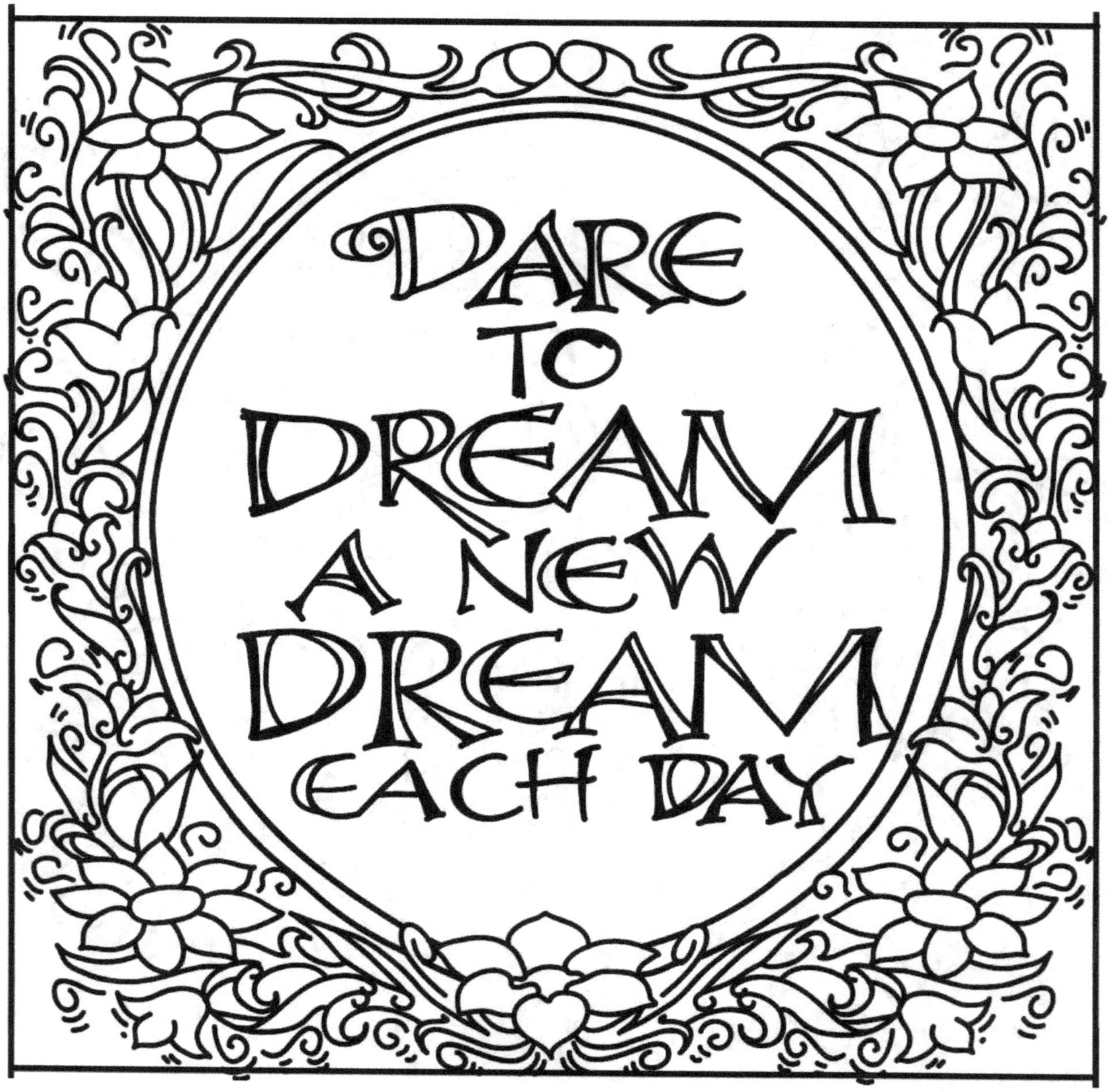
DARE
TO
DREAM
A NEW
DREAM
EACH DAY

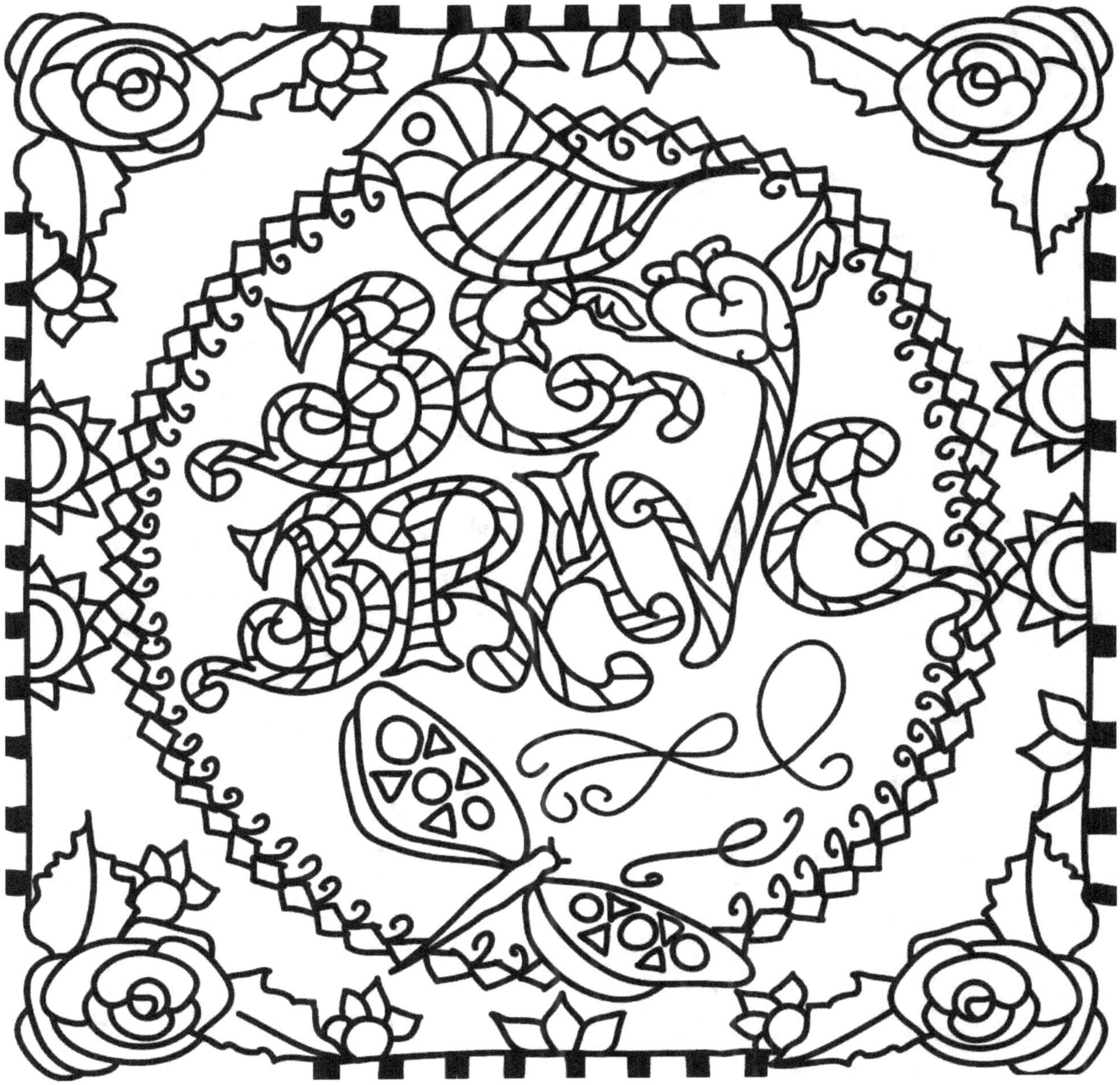
Be Brave

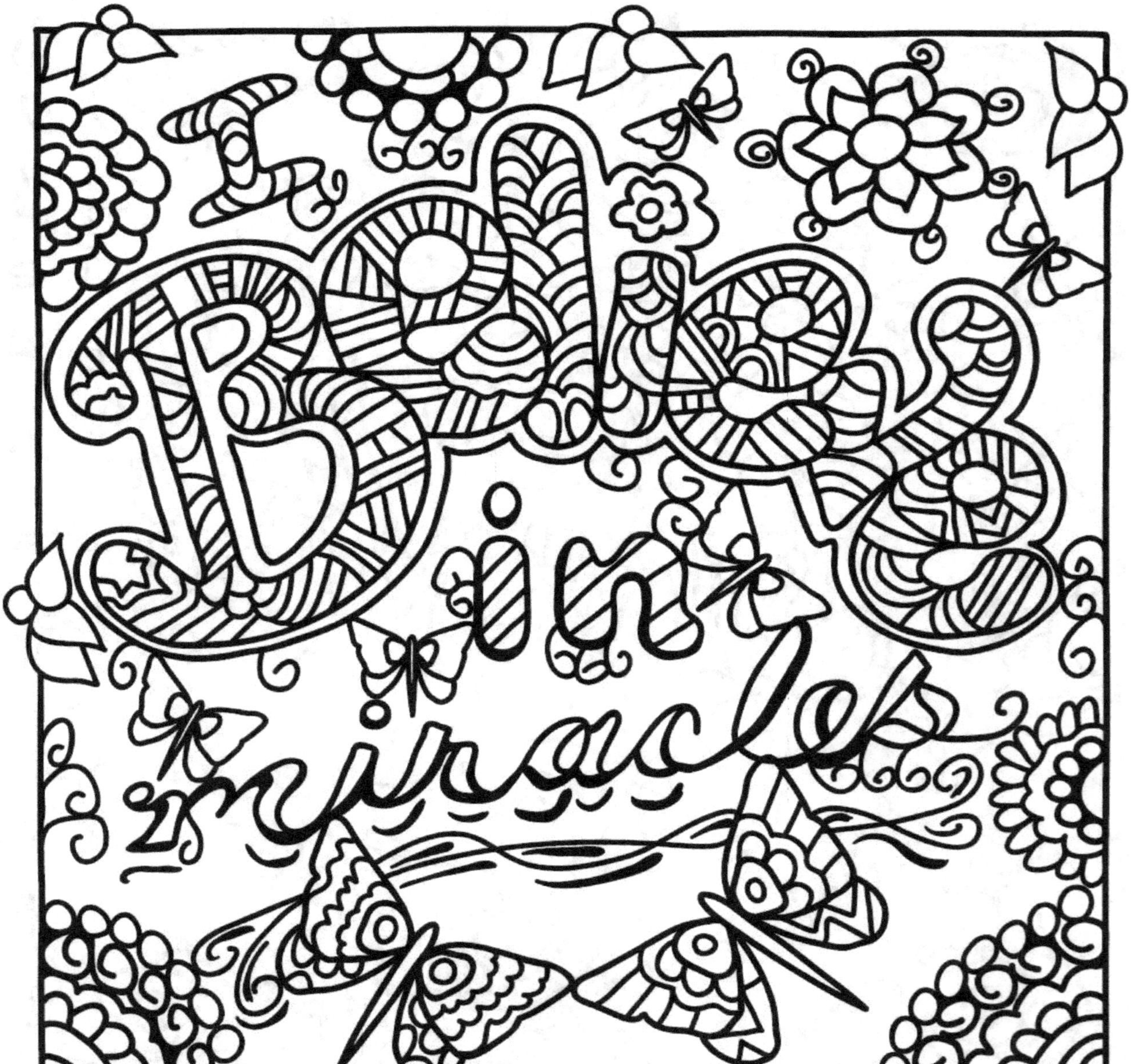
I Believe
in
miracles

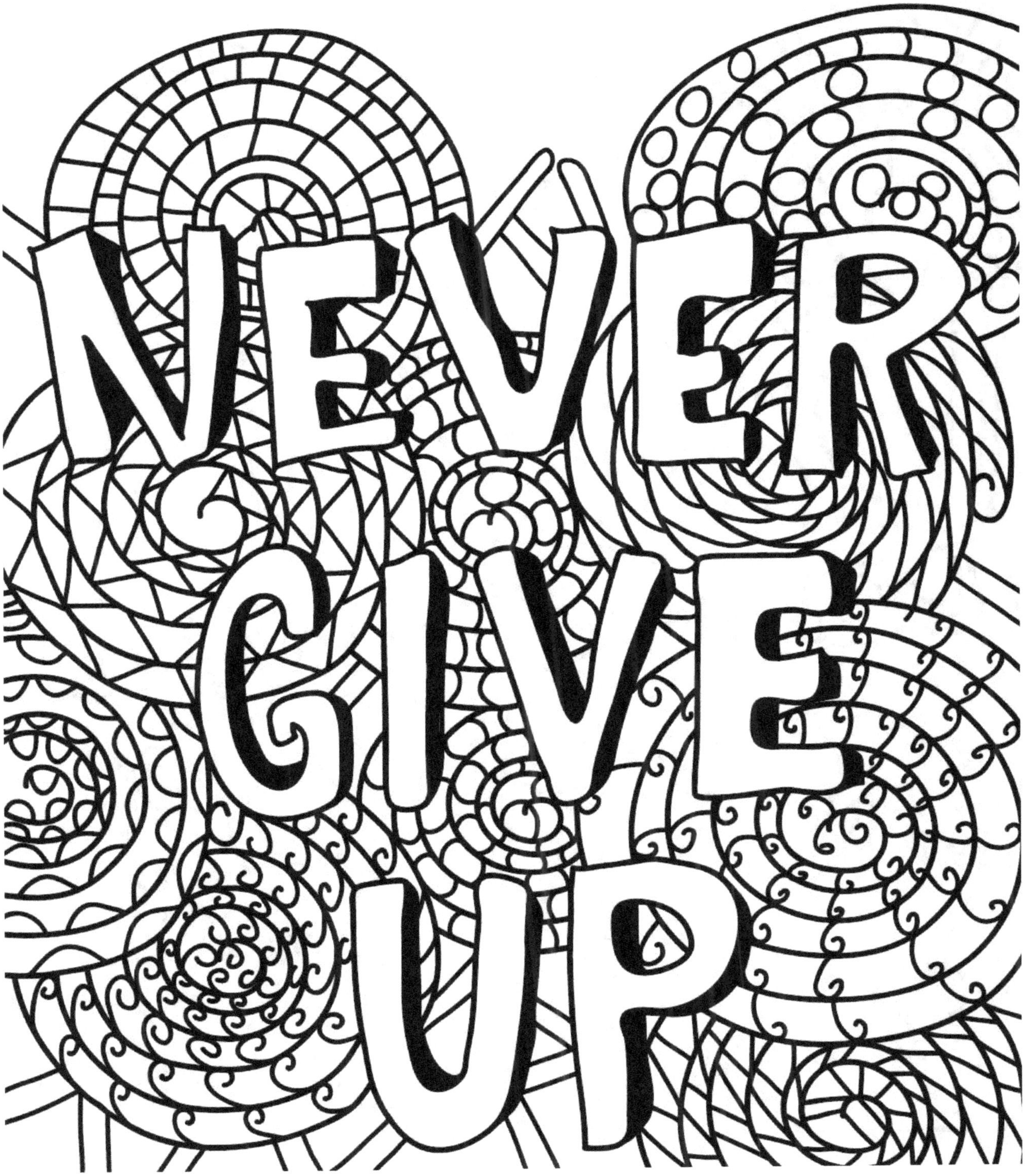
NEVER
GIVE
UP

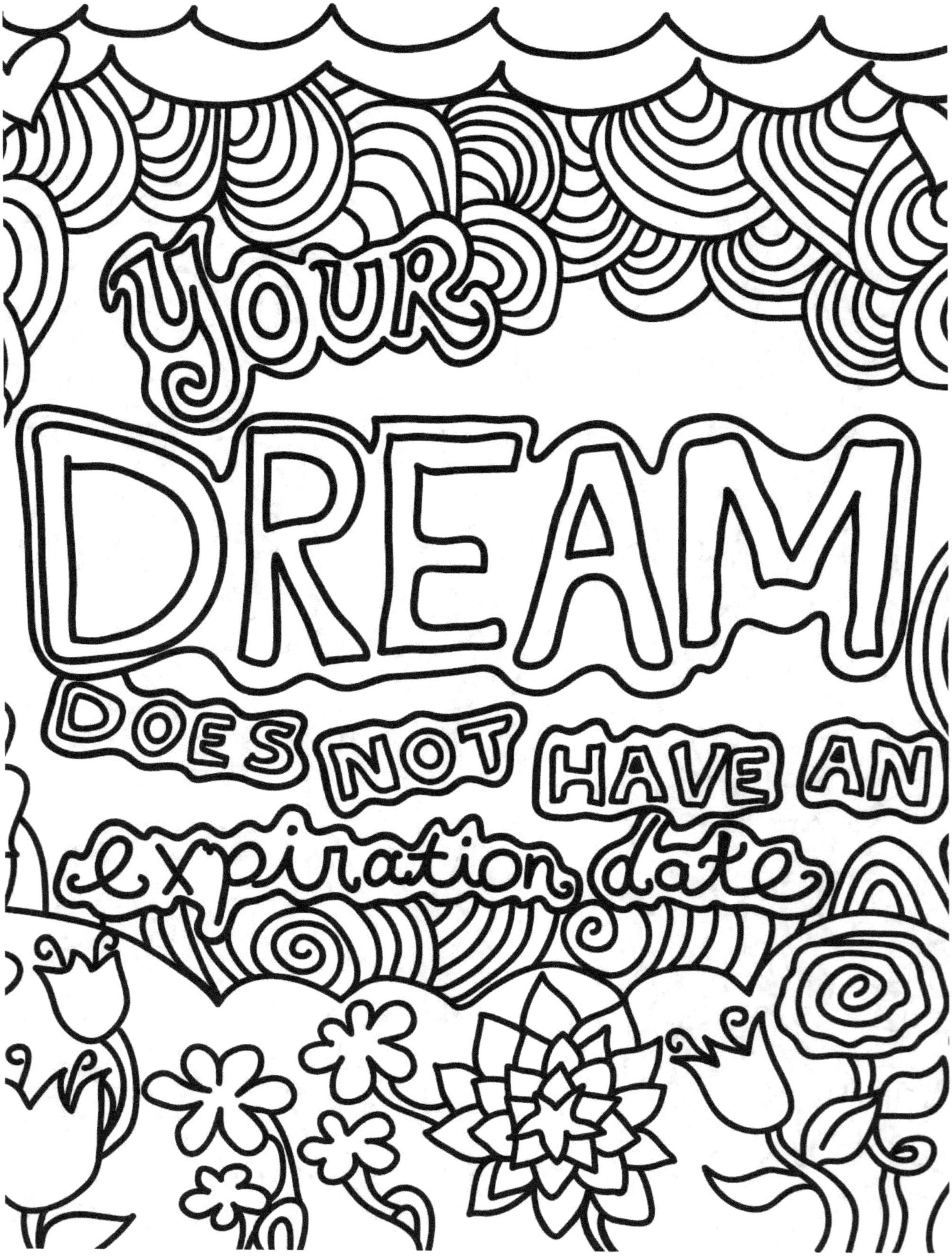
your
DREAM
DOES NOT HAVE AN
expiration date

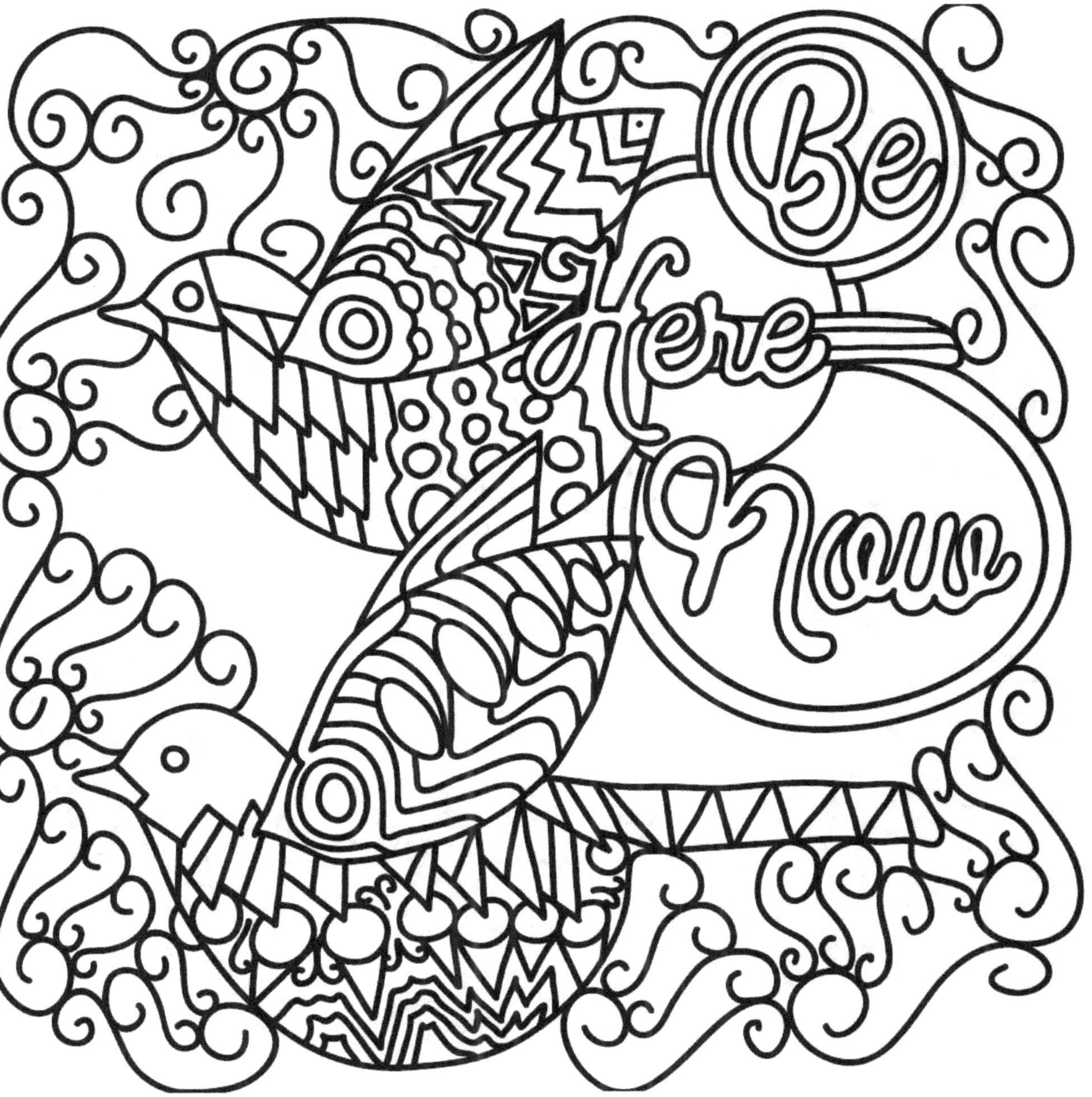
Be
Here
Now

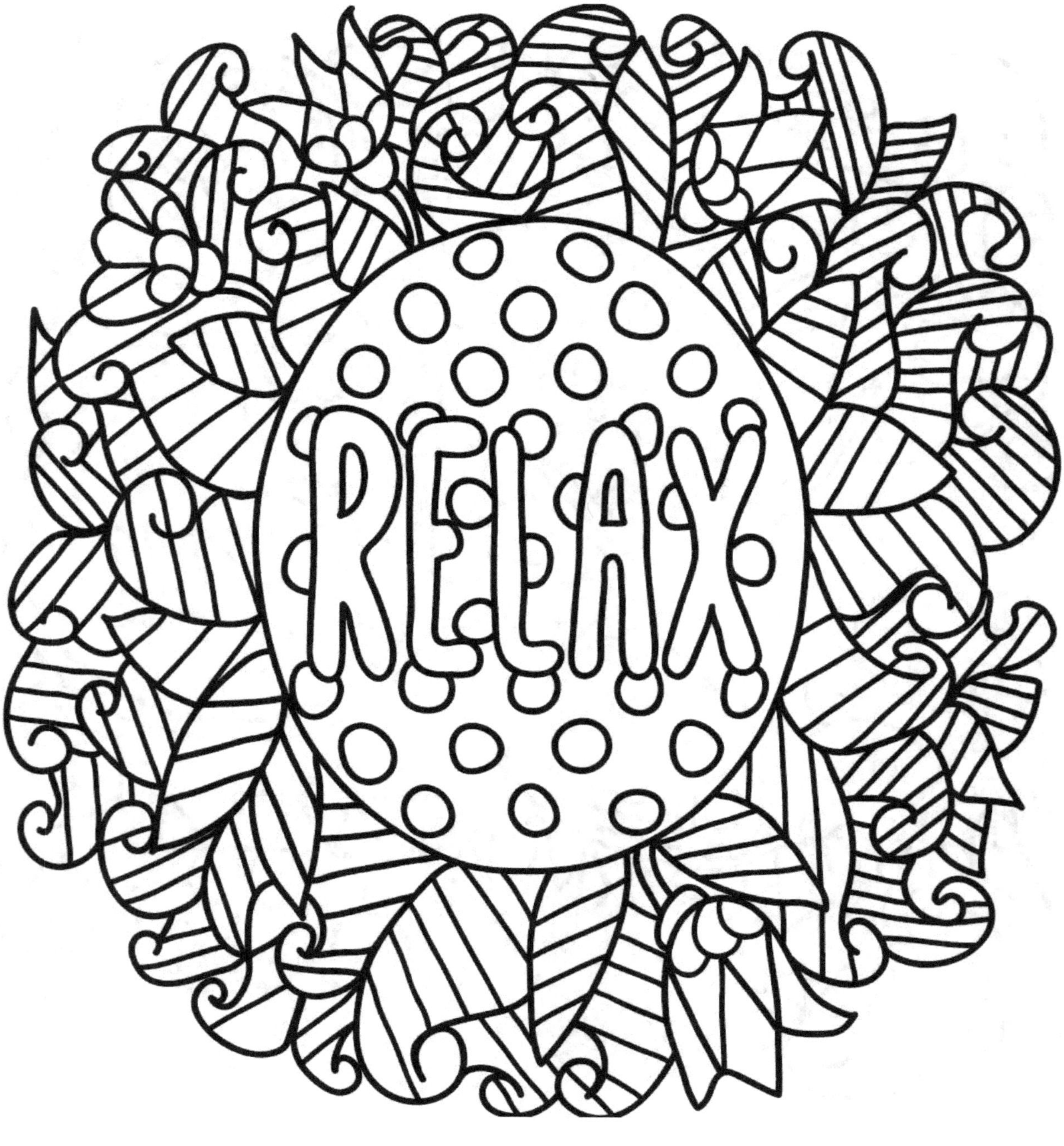
RELAX

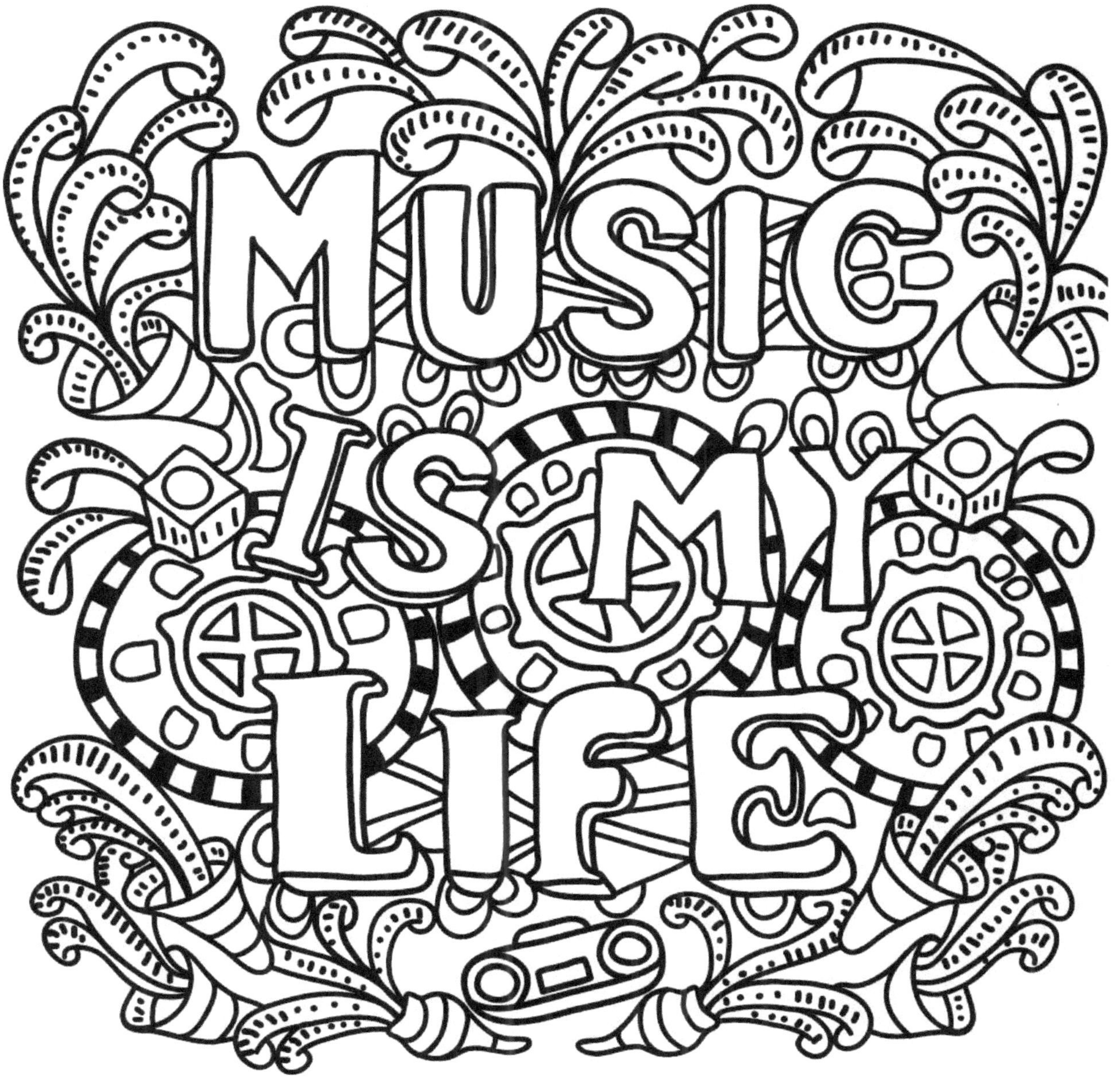
MUSIC
IS MY
LIFE